Curing and Smoking Fish

Stanley Marianski, Adam Marianski

Bookmagic LLC
Seminole, Florida

Curing and Smoking Fish
Stanley Marianski, Adam Marianski

ISBN: 978-0-9836973-9-8
Library of Congress Control Number: 2014906124

Bookmagic, LLC.
http://www.bookmagic.com

Printed in the United States of America.

Contents

Introduction

There are different brine strengths, brining times, smoking temperatures, smoking times and cooking times. To a newcomer, this can become confusing. We have tried to explain the art of smoking fish in simple practical terms, so that a reader can understand and control the entire process of preparing and smoking fish. You can approach the subject in two ways:

- Collect and follow blindly a collection of recipes, which will hardly make you an expert.
- Learn a few basic technical concepts and apply them in real situations.

We strongly promote the second approach which will make you an expert in no time at all. Take for example, a fish fillet. It can come from a lean or a fat fish, it can have skin or not, it can have skin with scales or not. The skin creates a barrier to salt, moisture and smoke penetration. The skin with scales will be almost impenetrable, but skin which is scorched with a razor blade will allow salt and smoke to go through. A hanging fillet will smoke faster than the one lying on the screen.

So, who decides how to prepare and process the fish? Yo do!

Fish can be dry salted or immersed in brine. The salt can be applied alone or with sugar and spices; the brine can be weak or strong, the fish can be cold or hot smoked, the wood chips can be dry or wet, there are many parameters to consider.

All such details are mentioned and explained so you can control the process with your own hands. Learn the basics, but don't be afraid to apply them in real applications. And never forget the most important rule: the fish is safe to eat when it has been thoroughly cooked. It can be more or less salty, it can have gold, light or dark brown color, it can be moist or dry, but it has to be safe to eat.

There is a discussion about smokehouses, methods of heating and generating smoke. In addition a set of plans is included for building a simple, but very practical smoker. Lastly, to get the reader started, there is a collection of recipes for smoking fish, making fish spreads and preparing sauces for serving fish.

Stanley Marianski

Chapter 1

Selecting Fish

Fish must be of good quality, plump, firm and of a pleasant smell. Fresh fish is the best material, however, frozen fish is acceptable. A quality product cannot be made from stale fish; heavy smoking may disguise the bad quality to some extent, but only for a day or two.

Using Frozen Fish

Freezing fish will not improve its quality, we can only hope to match the quality of the fresh material. Mark the date when the fish goes into the freezer. Try to freeze fish as fast as possible by making sure they have access to cold air and are not just lying on top of each other. In a day or two you can rearrange them the way you like. The fresh fish will have a firmer structure after smoking. The ice crystals which form during freezing inflict damage to fish tissues. and facilitate reaction between proteins, enzymes and meat.

There are differences between home and commercial refrigerators and freezers:

Home refrigerator	Butcher's cooler
36° - 40 F° (2° - 4° C)	32 F ° (0° C)
Home freezer	Butcher's freezer
0° F (-18° C)	-25° F (- 32° C)

During thawing there is a loss of meat juices, dissolved proteins, vitamins and minerals, especially when the freezing was slow. The resulting red liquid that we see on the plate during thawing meat is not blood, there may be some blood in it but the main portion constitutes meat juice.

Product	The maximum recommended times for freezing fish in months	
	0 F (-18 C)	-22 F (-30 C)
Fat fish	4	12
Lean fish	8	24
Shrimp and crab	6	15
Clams	4	12

Frozen fish loses weight as water evaporates through sublimation. What this means is that ice which is present in the surface area evaporates without going through the liquid phase. This problem, however, is of more importance for commercial producers as it results in a financial loss.

Meat products stored in freezer will start developing inferior taste due to the oxidation of fat. Those chemical changes known as "rancidity" occur spontaneously and are triggered by light or oxygen. Meats stored in a freezer will turn rancid more slowly than meats stored in a refrigerator. Rancid meat is noticeable more with frozen meat than chilled meat because bacteria can spoil meat in a refrigerator well before rancidity begins. To prevent fat oxidation and to prolong shelf life of the product, antioxidants such as BHA, BHT, TBHQ and rosemary extracts are commonly used. In the early days of industrial refrigeration the fish were often frozen in brine, however it contributed to faster oxidation of fats. Common vitamin C (ascorbic acid) slows down rancidity of fats. Adding 0.1% of orange essential oil will provide the same effect.

Fat Content

Fats carry the flavor and provide a pleasant mouth-feel. For these reasons fatty fish taste better when smoked. The same species of fish, depending where they live (Europe, Atlantic or Pacific Ocean), may have a significantly different fat content in their flesh which changes throughout the year.

Lean fish and shellfish: Cod family (cod, haddock, pollock, whiting), grouper, snapper, flatfish (flounder, sole, halibut), perch, pike, clams, scallops, tilapia, yellowfin tuna.

Semi-fat: mullet, salmon, trout.

Fat fish: bluefish, carp, eel, herring, mackerel, salmon.

All fish may be smoked, but *the fat fish absorb smoke better, stay moister during smoking and taste better.* This does not mean that lean fish cannot be smoked. The best example are the million pounds of haddock that have been smoked in England.

Photo 1.1 A great amount of fat is found under the skin along the lateral line where the flesh is much darker (see the arrows). Removing some of this flesh will decrease the fishy flavor of the fish.

Fat content of different fish		
Lean fish	less than 2.5%	
Medium fat fish	2.5 - 6.5%	best for smoking
Fat fish	more than 6.5%	best for smoking

The following table lists fat content of popular fish.

Fat Content of Different Fish

Name	Protein (%)	Fat (%)	Water (%)
Blue fish	20.04	4.24	70.86
Carp	17.83	5.60	76.31
Catfish	16.38	2.82	80.36
Clams	14.67	0.96	78.98
Cod, Atlantic	17.81	0.67	81.22
Cod, Pacific	15.27	0.41	83.95
Eel	18.44	11.66	68.26
Flounder (sole)	12.41	1.93	84.63
Grouper	19.38	1.02	79.22
Haddock	16.32	0.45	83.38
Halibut	18.56	1.33	80.34
Herring, Atlantic	17.96	9.04	72.05
Herring, Pacific	16.39	13.88	71.52
King Mackerel	20.28	2.00	75.85
Mackerel, Atlantic	18.60	13.89	63.55
Mackerel, Spanish	19.29	6.30	71.67
Mullet	19.35	3.79	77.01
Mussels	11.90	2.24	80.58
Oysters, Eastern	5.71	1.71	89.04
Oysters, Pacific	9.45	2.30	82.06
Salmon, Pink	20.50	4.40	75.52
Salmon, Atlantic, wild	19.84	6.34	68.50
Salmon, Atlantic, farmed	20.42	13.42	64.89
Scallops	12.06	0.49	82.53
Sheepshead	20.21	2.41	77.97
Shrimp	20.10	0.51	78.45
Snapper	20.51	1.34	76.87
Squid	15.58	1.38	78.55
Tilapia	20.08	1.70	78.08
Trout, rainbow, farmed	19.94	6.18	73.80
Tuna, yellowfin	24.00	0.49	74.03
Tuna, bluefin	23.00	4.90	68.09
Whiting	18.30	1.31	80.27

Data: U.S. Nutritional Database

Fish Flesh Color

Meat color is determined largely by the amount of *myoglobin* a particular animal carries. The more *myoglobin* the darker the meat. To some extent oxygen use can be related to the animal's general level of activity; muscles that are exercised frequently such as the legs need more oxygen. As a result they develop a darker color unlike the breast which is white due to little exercise. Fish float in water and need less muscle energy to support their skeletons.

Most fish meat is white, with some red meat around the fins, tail, and the more active parts of the fish which are used for swimming. Most fish don't have *myoglobin* at all. There are some antarctic cold water fish that have *myoglobin,* but it is confined to the hearts only (flesh of the fish remains white but the heart is of a rosy color). *The pink color of some fish, such as salmon and trout, is due to astaxanthin, a naturally occurring pigment in the crustaceans they eat.* Most salmon we buy is farm raised and as it is fed a prepared commercial diet that even includes antibiotics, its meat is anything but pink. The only reason that farmed raised salmon flesh is pink is that canthaxanthin (colorant) is added to the food the fish eats.

The pink color of smoked meat is due to the nitrite reaction with *myoglobin*. As most of the fish don't have *myoglobin* the meat is not going to be pink even if cured with nitrite and that explains why very few fish recipes include sodium nitrite. In addition, nitrites are not allowed in all species of fish used for smoking. The Food and Drug Administration currently allows nitrites to be used in salmon, sablefish, shad, chubs, and tuna.

Why out of millions of species of fish swimming in the ocean, only five species can be cured with nitrite? What made those fish so special? A letter of inquiry was sent to the Food Safety and Inspection Service and this was the answer:

"The reason nitrite is approved for use in those species is because someone submitted a petition for its use in those specific fish. Other species can be added through additional petitions."

Some red- flesh fish such as mackerel or jack may have dark muscles that will become blackish-red after processing. Such fish will benefit from curing them with salt and sodium nitrite (cure #1) to preserve their red color.

Shellfish

Shellfish is a family of animals that include:

1. Molluscs *(clams, mussels, oysters and scallops)* are the most smoked shellfish. In *bivalves* such as *clams, mussels, oysters, scallops* the soft body parts are enclosed between two shells and a powerful muscle brings them together; hence, the word bivalve.

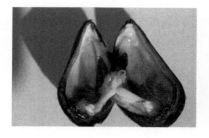

Photo 1.2 Blue mussel.   **Photo 1.3** Littleneck clam.

Photo 1.4 Oyster.

Conch, also known as abalone is a popular item in the Caribbean, especially Bahamas, it is also found in Florida. The conch shell is probably the most popular shell in the world.

Photo 1.5 Conch.   **Photo 1.6** Conch.

Limpet is a common name applied to a group of sea snails, marine gastropod molluscs which have a simple broadly conical shell that, unlike the shell of most snails, is not coiled. Seasnails are edible, although their texture is somewhat rubbery.

Photo 1.7 Seasnails.

Cephalopods (squid and octopus)

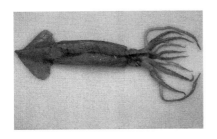

Photo 1.8 Squid.

2. Crustaceans - crabs, lobsters, crayfish, shrimp, krill and barnacles.

Photo 1.9 Shrimp.

3. Echinoderms – starfish, sea urchin, sand dollars, sea cucumbers.

Photo 1.10 Seabiscuit.

Shellfish contain significant amount of carbohydrates:

Shellfish	Carbohydrates (%)
Mussels	3.69
Oysters, eastern	2.72
Oysters, eastern, farmed	5.53
Scallops	3.18
Squid	3.08

Photo 1.11 Smoked clams, mussels, shrimp and scallops with cocktail sauce and garlic and curry butters.

Safety Considerations

After the fish has died, the enzymes which are present in the gut, digest the walls of the intestinal tract and start spoiling the flesh. Most of the bacteria are present in the *slime* that covers the body of the fish, *the gills and in its digestive tract*. The skin produces this slime to protect the fish from the outside bacteria and to decrease the resistance of water when swimming. When the fish dies, its skin releases more slime which becomes an ideal substrate for bacteria to multiply. They start penetrating the skin and the spoiling process begins.

Fish can be the source of the following diseases: *Salmonella, Shigella, Staphylococcus aureus* (known as "stuff" infection), *Cl. perfringens* and *Cl. botulinum*. The last one is hardest to eliminate, and is commonly known as "food poisoning." *Cl. botulinum* is not associated with fish only, but with all low acid foods such as meats, poultry and vegetables. Canning industry safety procedures are based on elimination of *Cl. botulinum* spores using reasoning that "if the procedure can kill *Clostridium botulinum spores*, it will kill all other microorganisms as well."

Fish like any other meat is susceptible to food poisoning given the right conditions for the development of *C. Botulinum* spores into toxins. Those conditions (lack of oxygen, humidity, temperatures 40-140° F(4-60° C) always exist when smoking meats. Furthermore many times fish will be packed by the Reduced Oxygen Packaging Method that can create favorable conditions for *C.botulinum* to become toxin even after fish was hot smoked and cooked. To eliminate the possibility of such a danger cure # 1 is added the same way it is used when smoking meats or sausages. The Food and Drug Administration currently allows nitrites to be used in salmon, sablefish, shad, chubs, and tuna

Adapted from Torry Notes #22, Torry Research Station, UK.:

Botulism in Fishery Products

What is Botulism?

Botulism is an often fatal food poisoning disease caused by one of the most powerful toxins known to man. A toxin is a poison produced by certain bacteria when they grow on food; the kind of bacterium that forms the toxin causing botulism is called *Clostridium botulinum*. When food containing the toxin is eaten, the nervous system is affected and death can follow within hours.

Clostridium Botulinum in Fish

There are seven known types of *Clostridium botulinum*, referred to as types A-G; of these, A, B, E and F consistently produce botulism in humans, and B, E and F are frequently found in the sea. *Clostridium botulinum* grows only in the **absence of oxygen,** and type E, and some varieties of B and F, have two important properties. First, they are found in **fish intestines and gills** and in mud from the sea, whereas the other types are found mostly in soil. Secondly, they grow and form toxin at a much lower temperature than the other types; they can grow at 41° F (5°C) in fish products. Fortunately the toxin is readily destroyed by cooking since it does not survive exposure to 158° F (70° C) for 2 minutes.

Over the years public taste has changed and with it the methods of curing. At one time the product was *so heavily salted, smoked and dried that Clostridium botulinum, where present in fish, could not grow and produce toxin.* Such a heavily cured product needed to be neither refrigerated nor vacuum packed during distribution. Nowadays hot-smoked fish are distributed with much less smoke and salt, and much more moisture, with the result that any *Clostridium botulinum* present can more readily form toxin when the fish are kept warm for some length of time.

Smoked Fish and Botulism

Salmon flesh is either dry salted or brined before being *cold smoked*, the time of salting varying with the size of salmon being cured. The presence of salt in the product has a great effect on the growth of *Clostridium botulinum*, but the concentration of salt in smoked salmon is not usually high enough to prevent growth altogether; commercial smoked salmon usually contains 1 to 4 percent salt. The concentration required to prevent growth at room temperature can vary from as low as 3 percent to 5 percent or more, so that the amount of salt present in smoked salmon on its own is no guarantee against the danger of botulism. Trout and mackerel are brined and then *hot smoked*, either as gutted whole fish or as fillets. The range of salt concentration is similar to that found in salmon.

How to Control Botulism

Before the toxin of *Clostridium botulinum* can develop in fish products a number of factors must coincide: the organism must be present in the fish, the time and temperature of storage must be favorable for toxin production, and the chemical composition of the product must be such that it supports the growth of the organism. Elimination of any one of these factors will make the product safe.

In practice it is not possible to rid a contaminated fish of botulinum organisms but *removal of the guts and gills, followed by thorough washing of the belly cavity with tap water, can reduce contamination by as much as 90 percent.*

Parasites

Wild fish are infected with a large variety of parasites which can infect a person that likes to eat raw or lightly preserved fish such as sashimi, sushi, ceviche, and gravlax (salted salmon). Parasites can attach themselves to fish body, penetrate its flesh or settle down in the gills or the liver. They are not a health concern in thoroughly cooked fish. Raw fish should be frozen to an internal temperature of −4°F (−20°C) for at least 7 days to kill parasites. It is important to be aware that many home freezers are not cold enough to kill parasites.

Summary

The bacteria can grow at a temperature as low as 38° F (3.3°C) but its toxin is destroyed by heating it at 70°C; any product that is properly cooked and eaten the same day is therefore safe; *the main danger lies in products that either can be eaten raw*, such as smoked salmon, or *need not be cooked* by the consumer, for example hot-smoked fish.

Changes in traditional method of processing can introduce new hazards; for example, reduction in the amount of salt or smoke can allow bacteria to flourish, or the use of vacuum packs can extend the shelf life of the product sufficiently to allow the product to become toxic during storage.

The safety of any product is assured if the fish are stored at a chill temperature below 4°C from the time they are caught until they are eaten.

The fish is considered safe to consume when submitted to 145° F (63° C) inside temperature for 30 minutes.

The U.S. Food and Drug Administration **"Good Manufacturing Practice"** for "hot smoked fish" recommends that *commercially* prepared smoked fish be subjected to one of the following:

Center temperature must reach at least 180° F (82 C) for 30 minutes if water phase salt (WPS) content is a minimum of 3.5% OR

Center temperature must reach at least 105° F (41° C) for 30 minutes if water phase salt content is a minimum of 5%. Without chemical analysis it is hard to tell what is the WPS content of the fish, however, *most 1 to 2 inch thick pieces of fish will reach these conditions* if salted 1-2 hours in 60 SAL brine (15.8% salt by weight) and smoked for 4-5 hours at 180-200° F (82-94° C), followed by 4-8 hours of smoking without heat.

Guidance for Processing Seafood in Retail Operations states that:

Cold Smoked Seafood – seafood that has been produced by subjecting the product to mild heat and smoke to achieve a partial coagulation of proteins.

Oven/smoker temperature not to exceed 90° F (32.2° C), for a drying and smoking period that does not exceed 20 hours; OR

Oven/smoker temperature not to exceed 50° F, (10° C), for a drying and smoking period not to exceed 24 hours.

Hot Smoked Seafood – smoked seafood that has been produced by subjecting the product to heat during the smoking process to coagulate the proteins throughout the seafood.

Product internal temperature must be maintained at a continuous temperature of at least 145° F (62.8° C), for a minimum of 30 minutes.

Chapter 2

Cleaning Fish

Cleaning fish can be intimidating to many newcomers. There are different fish, and although they may follow the basic anatomical structure, nevertheless there are differences. Flounder, perch, trout, eel, mullet, all of these are fish, yet they are gutted differently. Cleaning fish does not conform to rigid rules as applied to chicken, pork or beef. Those animals may come in different colors, however the skeleton and organ placement remains the same for each animal, regardless of its origin. Preparing seafood products can be confusing, take for example mollusks which belong to seashell family. You have clams and mussels, oysters, shrimp, lobster, squid; they all look different and are prepared accordingly.

The methods of cleaning a fish are as varied as the individual fisherman. The *gills and guts* of a fish should be removed a soon as possible since they contain the highest concentration of bacteria that cause spoilage. How the fish is processed depends on the planned method of cooking and the size of the fish. Whole fish is certainly easier to clean, hang and smoke, however, it is less appetizing to the eater. There are people who don't eat fish not because of the flavor, but because they hate playing with fish bones. Well, for them nothing will work, but the fillet. So, to a large extent, the choice of the cleaning method is dictated by by the amount of work you are willing to dedicate to the project.

It makes little sense to fillet a small fish as there would not be much left to eat and the fish would be wasted. Small fish should be left whole or split in "butterfly" version which is typical of mullet. Bigger, especially thicker fish like cod, red drum, halibut, sheepshead, king mackerel or jack can be filleted. Very large fish, for example swordfish or tuna are usually cut across into steaks.

But, what do you do with a big jack?

Photo 2.1 Adam Marianski with big jack.

Photo 2.2 Very large fish like tuna or the jack above, are usually cut into steaks.

Photo 2.3 Small jacks are thick   **Photo 2.4** Filleted jack.
enough for filleting.

Whole fish should first be washed to remove slime, loose scales and traces of blood. Then they are beheaded (if required) and gutted. Washing removes slime, traces of blood and small particles that would otherwise cling to the fish. The belly cavity should be cleaned, some fish contain black belly wall lining which should be removed. The gills, entrails and all traces of blood are removed, especially the bloody kidney line along the back of the fish. The fish should be washed again before brining them. If fillets are cut, they should be trimmed and be reasonably free from blemishes. When filleting fat fish, it is recommended to leave the skin on as a significant amount of fat is deposited between the skin and the flesh. In lean fish, for example cod, the skin can be be removed. Previously frozen fish can be thawed in a refrigerator or under cold running water.

The following procedures and photos describe how to prepare Florida mullet for smoking, however, they can be applied to other fish as well.

Mullet is not a huge fish, averaging about one foot in length and just over one pound in weight. You can occasionally catch bigger individuals, up to 24 inches long and weighing 2-3 pounds. Those are better suited for filleting.

Mullet is a semi-fat fish and tasted great when smoked. The fish has a strong skin and quite large scales, which can be removed or not. Large fish can be filleted. The tender flesh tends to fall apart when the skin is removed so leave the skin on when smoking. The fish has an oily layer between the skin and its flesh and this oil makes mullet tender and juicy.

Dressing Mullet "Butterfly" Style

Mullet is usually split open "butterflied" or gutted and left whole. In both cases the head is cut off and the entrails are removed. Scaling is messy but you can place the fish inside of a trash bag and scrape off the scales. They will fly left and right so the best idea is to do it outside. Any dull knife, spoon or proper fish scaler will do the job, just make sure that the scales are wet. *Wet scales come off much easier than dry ones.*

Photo 2.5 Cutting the head off.

Photo 2.6 A larger mullet has a stronger backbone and sometimes the knife will not cut through it. You can easily break the fish in two.

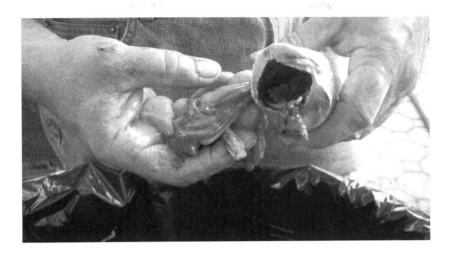

Photo 2.7 Gently squeeze the body of the fish and all entrails can be removed with your fingers. It is much easier than it looks.

You may keep edible parts such as gizzard or roe. Mullet and shad are the only fish that have gizzards. These can be fried up just like chicken gizzards. With a little hot sauce they're wonderful.

Photo 2.8 There are no entrails left, the black stomach lining can easily be brushed away.

Photo 2.9 Scrape scales with knife, scaler tool or a spoon from the tail towards the front. Scaling can be done at any time, before the fish is gutted or after. It is easier to remove scales when they are wet.

Photo 2.10 Make the incision from the back towards the belly over the backbone. Don't cut through the belly.

Photo 2.11 The back is split but the belly remains intact.

Photo 2.12 Continue cutting through the rib cage towards the vent. *The belly is not cut.* Come out with the knife through the vent, cutting towards the tail and cutting above the backbone.

Photo 2.13 Continue cutting to the tail.

Photo 2.14 Split mullet "butterfly" style. The belly is intact.

Photo 2.15 The stomach lining is covered with black film which is easily brushed and hosed away.

Photo 2.16 The kidney line runs along the backbone and it must be removed. It is bitter and will promote the growth of bacteria. It can be scraped with a brush or even your finger, then rinsed away.

Photo 2.17 Clean mullet.

Dressing Whole Mullet

Photo 2.18 Head is cut off and the entrails are removed.

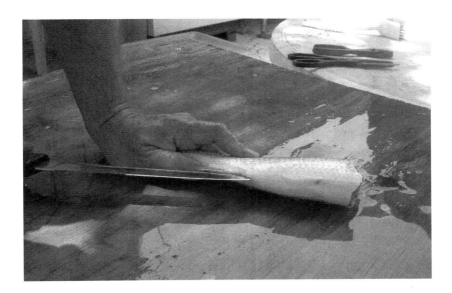

Photo 2.19 The knife is inserted into the vent.

Photo 2.20 The belly is cut towards the front.

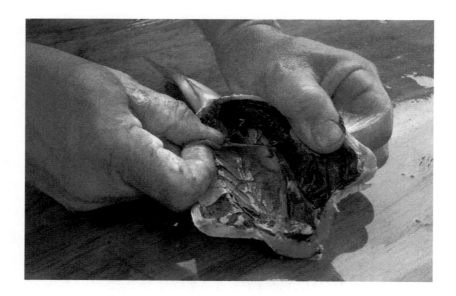

Photo 2.21 The stomach liner.

Photo 2.22 Stomach liner and the kidney line are brushed away.

Photo 2.23 The fish is rinsed.

Photo 2.24 Clean whole mullet.

Filleting

The main part of the flesh of a fish constitute the body muscles, two dorsal and two ventral muscles on each side separated from one another by strong connective tissue along the lateral line.

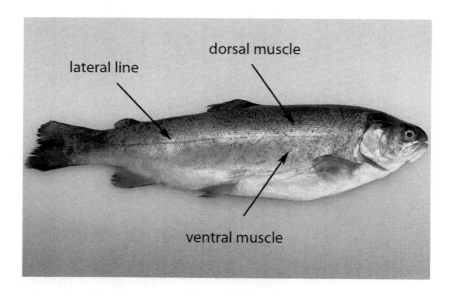

Photo 2.25 The main muscles of the fish.

Remember that the ventral muscle is covering the rib cage in the front of the fish and is much thinner there. It becomes thicker again as it passes the vent towards the tail.

Some sources recommend removing scales, others ask to leave them on. Scales act as a tough barrier and removing scales provides the following benefits:

- Faster salt penetration during brining.
- Faster smoke penetration.
- The product develops better gloss and looks more appealing.

Use only meaty fish for filleting. Supermarkets sell frozen fish fillets but they are often packaged in a way that prevents seeing the contents. The bag that weighs one pound may contain many thin fillets. Keep in mind that a fillet will loose a lot of moisture during smoking and cooking. A thin fillet will become so thin after smoking that it may be difficult to handle.

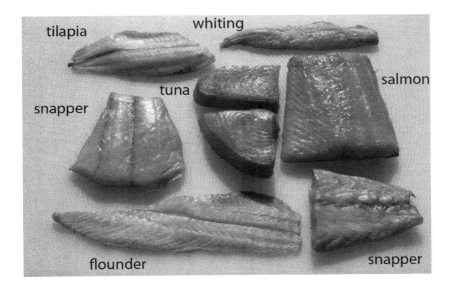

Photo 2.26 The flounder fillet is much thinner than the tuna or salmon.

You can leave the skin on fat fish fillets like mullet, salmon, mackerel, trout, eel or bluefish. Fat fish have substantial amount of fat under their skins and this skin can be easily peeled of after smoking. The skin of lean fish such as cod, whiting, flounder, tilapia will adhere to the flesh very tightly after smoking and will be hard to remove. You may consider to remove the skin from lean fish fillets prior to smoking. Make sure that the screen is oiled to prevent fillets from sticking.

A lighter-flavored fillet can be produced by deep skinning the fish and discarding the underside layer of the skin. The disadvantage is that even a skilled operator must throw away a lot of usable meat that is located around the backbone.

Sheepshead, also known as the "convict" fish is often caught along with mullet. The filleting procedure for both fish is the same, however, sheepshead fillets are thicker.

Photo 2.27 Sheepshead. **Photo 2.28** A cut is made around the gill cover. There is no need to cut off the head or gut the fish when filleting.

Photo 2.29 A cut is made on the top side of the fish as close to the backbone as possible. Make sure that the knife is sharp and take your time.

Photo 2.30 The knife separates flesh from the skin using a sawing motion. On the underside of the skin you can find a red and oily layer of flesh. This is where most of the fish flavor is present.

Photo 2.31 and Photo 2.32 The hardest part is to cut over the rib cage. It is difficult to feel the rib cage when a fish is small.

Photo 2.33 Filleted fish.

Gibbing

The entrails can be removed without cutting fish. This procedure is often used for baking stuffed fish and is known as *gibbing*.

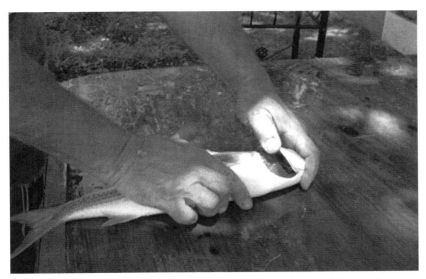

Photo 2.34 The entrails will be removed through the gill opening.

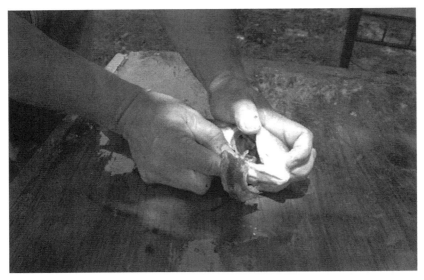

Photo 2.35 Gills can be removed with fingers. Knife or scissors may be needed on a larger fish.

Photo 2.36 Then all the guts can be pulled out.

Photo 2.37 A long and stiff toothbrush will scrape off the stomach lining and the red kidney line.

Photo 2.38 Fully dressed mullet which was not cut at all. Such a fish can be stuffed, baked and served elegantly on a plate.

Cutting the Chin

The fastest way to gut most fish is by cutting off the head and splitting the belly. However, for visual effects, we may want the head to be attached to the body. The gills and the entrails can be removed by cutting into the area under the chin that joins the bottom of the two gill openings. Then cut the belly cavity without cutting the intestinal tract. Now, the gills and entrails can be pulled out. Trout which is sold in supermarkets is prepared that way. This can be further simplified by splitting the belly from the vent forward. Many fish can be prepared this way, although some rock fish have such hard jaws that the method becomes impractical.

Photo 2.39 This trout has been gutted by cutting the chin and removing gills and entrails through its mouth.

Photo 2.40 This is the same fish presented in the figure above.

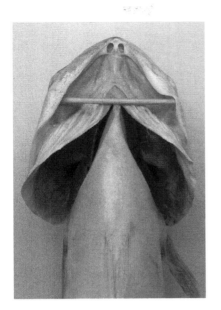

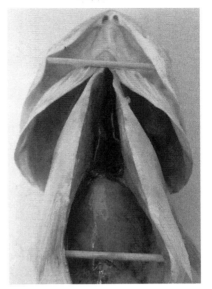

Photo 2.41 The uncut fish.

Photo 2.42 This is the same fish presented in the figure above.

Photo 2.43 Cutting the chin membrane.

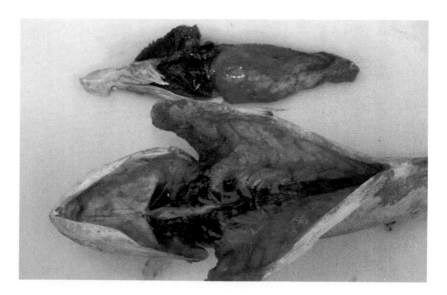

Photo 2.44 After the chin membrane has been cut, the gills with attached entrails are removed.

Photo 2.45 The body cavity is washed and all traces of blood are removed.

Bleeding Fish

Bleeding fish is a phrase used to describe the removal of blood from fish. It should be performed as soon as possible when the fish are caught. Bleeding fish is performed to preserve the quality and appearance of the meat. Mullet are bled by snapping the head off the body then sticking the index finger and middle fingers in their gills and ripping them out. The blood immediately starts to squirt out for about 10 seconds. There are a few main advantages to bleeding mullet: it results in whiter meat when filleted, there is a less fishy flavor present, and the bacteria spoilage is slowed down.

Photo 2.46 Bled mullet.

Some fish have little scales, in others the number will vary, for example European King Carp have a few scales on top, but wild carp is fully covered with them. Scales can be removed with a scale removing scraper or back of the knife going from the tail toward the head. The scales will fly everywhere so the operation is best performed outside or by placing the fish in a large plastic bag.

Processing a Large Fish Catch

If you catch 50 or more fish at the time, you have to properly plan your cleaning operation. A hose with running water and a stiff nylon brush are needed. It will take hours to process so many fish, so large containers filled with ice are needed.

Note: if the fish will be brined, don't forget to prepare the brine a day earlier and keep it in a refrigerator or freezer. Salty water (brine) freezes at a lower temperature than fresh water. Large amounts of brine kept in a freezer overnight will develop only a little ice on top. The disadvantage of preparing brine in the last moment is that it will not be cold, unless large amounts of ice are added to the water. This makes determining the strength of the brine much harder, besides it consumes valuable time that should be dedicated to processing fish. If the brine is not cold, the fish starts to spoil faster and its shelf life will be shorter.

Photo 2.47 Two gallons of 80° SAL brine are kept in a freezer to be prepared for any unexpected fish catch.

Photo 2.48 A nice catch of 63 mullet, 2 sheepshead, 1 tilapia and a blue crab. The fish were caught at night with a cast net from a little bridge in St. Petersburg, Florida.

Photo 2.49 A job of this size must be well organized: water hose, ice, large covered containers, table, garbage can, brush, knives, paper towels, etc.

Photo 2.50 Freshly caught and cleaned fish are *always kept on ice* until ready for brining. There are too many fish to transfer directly from the cleaning station to the brining container as the first ones will remain in the brine too long becoming overly salty.

Chapter 3

Curing Fish

Origins of Fish Curing

Fish salting was practiced for thousands of years. England and Norway derived a large portion of income by selling cured herring, cod and salmon to Southern European countries. Fish was traded for olive oil, wine and dry fruit; products which would not grow in cold climate. Discovery of America in 1492 by Christopher Columbus has given a way to trade. Spain was busy conquering islands and countries in South America, but England followed the shortest route and started to establish new settlements on Northern Atlantic coast, first in Newfoundland, then in New England.

The early colonists would not have been able to survive without protein rich food like the salted cod or smoked herring as the climate was harsh and the soil was poor. But the fish was plentiful and cured fish became their main source of income. Salt cod, salmon, smoked herring, halibut, and pickled sturgeon were soon exported to Europe. The cold climate was perfect for transporting salt fish to Europe, according to records, in 1580 more than 300 ships from Europe were engaged in salting cod in this area. This trade in salt fish stimulated further trade and growth in other industries. There was plenty of timber and local manufacturing starting to flourish. This led to more trade and more shipping lines.

Curing fish was the main preservation method until Nicholas Appert invented the canning process in 1810. This was followed by discovery of electricity and from 1900 and on, canning and refrigeration became popular preservation methods. These methods were more economical and produced food of higher quality and less spoilage.

Changing food habits have also contributed to decline in curing methods. European immigrants brought meat curing and smoking technology to America, but their children developed different food habits. Most foods today are prepared by either canning, drying or refrigerated. Keep in mind that every quality ham, sausage or smoked fish is always mildly cured, regardless of whether it is produced in a factory or at home. Commercial producers may use specialized machines to make the process faster, but a hobbyist can produce even better product at home. The curing process, however, remains the same as it has been for centuries.

England was always known and respected for the quality of their smoked fish. Torry Research Station, a division of the Department of Scientific and Industrial Research, designed the Torry Kiln (a mechanical fish smoking kiln) in 1939, which has been widely adopted by the fish smoking industry. They have also printed "Fish Smoking-A Torry Kiln Operator's Handbook", an excellent manual about smoking fish. Detailed instructions were given for the preparation of the typical smoke-cured products. In all the examples 80 degrees strong brine was used and this brine strength has become very popular.

Curing Fish

Prior to smoking, fish are either dry salted or brined. They may be lightly or heavily brined depending upon the type of product to be prepared. Lightly salted fish should be smoked immediately since the brining merely imparts a desirable flavor and firms the flesh. The salt content of the flesh of hot smoked fish should be about 1.8-2%, which corresponds to salt content in most smoked sausages. Heavy brining is used in the mild curing of salmon and for preserving fish until smoking can be applied. Such a fish must be soaked prior to smoking to remove most of the salt.

Curing by Salting Alone

Man was able to catch large number of fish, regardless of their size, the problem was how to preserve the catch. Salting fish was one of the first preservation methods, however, the fish had to be desalted for a few days before cooking started. Salting and drying fish is practiced today only in remote areas without access to electricity.

Light salting and brines are used for fish that would be immediately smoked. After brining, the fish is briefly rinsed and submitted to drying. The salt concentration is usually below 2%. Majority of hot smoked fish falls in this category.

Heavy salting and brines are used to prepare fish for cold smoking or to preserve the fish until the smoking process can be applied. The salt concentration reaches 8-10%. Preserved fish is kept in closed barrels until processing time. Such heavily cured fish is soaked in cold water to bring the salt content down. Cold running water will be most effective, standing water will need a few changes. Then the fish can be cooked or cold smoked.

Brining (Wet Curing)

All fish for hot smoking are brined to give them flavour. The recommended brine strength for most products is 80°, a stronger brine reduces the brining time but has the disadvantage that, after the fish are dried, salt crystallizes on the surface of the skin in unattractive white patches. Salt is absorbed more uniformly by fish in brine weaker than 80°, but residence time is longer; an 80° brine is a practical compromise.

After brining, whole fish are hung, for example on tenters or speats depending on the product and arranged in a smokehouse so that either the backs or the bellies, not the sides, of the fish face the smoke flow. Fillets and small products like shellfish meats are laid on wire mesh trays.

Brining provides the following advantages:

- Improves the flavor and looks of the fish.
- Improves texture by making flesh much stronger which is important if the fish is hung.
- Prevents growth of bacteria.
- Develops skin gloss (best with 70-80° brine).

Brine Strength

There is no one universal brine that may be applied to all fish. The composition of the brine depends on the fish type, thickness of the fillet or the size of the fish and the fattiness of the fish. If the flesh is not very thick most of the salt enters within the first 3 or 4 minutes. Salt is absorbed more uniformly by weaker brines, but the brining time is longer. The advantage of a stronger brine is that it is more effective at inhibiting bacteria growth. Typical brines:

Product	Brine Strength in ° Salinometer
Poultry	21
Loin	30
Pork butts, hams	40-50
Hot Smoked Fish	70-80
Cold Smoked Fish	80-90
The strength of seawater is 14°.	

Salt (cups)	Water (1 gallon)	Brine Strength in SAL degrees
1	1 gal	27
2	1 gal	45
3	1 gal	72
3.5	1 gal	80
4	1 gal	90

The recommended brine for most fish is 70-80 degrees, a brine stronger than 90° may leave salt crystal deposits on the skin of the fish, what will leave unattractive permanent white patches. Heavy brine can be used to preserve the fish until the smoking process can be applied. After a successful catch you may not have sufficient time to smoke all fish the same day. Clean and gut the fish, place them in a heavy brine - this will buy you time. Then a few days later, when you have time on the weekend, the fish can be desalted (soaked) and smoked. Fish can be heavily or lightly brined depending on the required product. A large fish and fat fish absorb salt slowly. Stronger brines require a shorter time of brining. Lightly salted fish can be smoked immediately since the brining was used merely to firm the flesh. Brine becomes weaker with use, however, this is of lesser importance in home production. Water on the surface of the fish dilutes the brine and the fish absorbs some salt. Commercial plant maintains the strength of the brine by adding more salt. As miniscule pieces of fish, gut, scales, blood start to contaminate the brine, the brine should be changed daily. Let's make something absolutely clear - smoked fish needs salt. This can be accomplished by sprinkling fish with salt or immersing fish in salty brine. All other ingredients may influence the flavor of smoked fish, but only a little. Those ingredients may as well be added to the fish during a meal. In addition you can serve fish with one of many classic sauces, which will influence the flavor of the fish much more than adding pepper, sugar or lime to brine. Those ingredients will release their flavor better when brining times are longer, but you have to decrease the strength of the brine, or the fish will end up too salty.

One gallon of brine is sufficient for 4-5 pounds of fish. Other ingredients like sugar and spices may be added to the solution after the correct brine strength has been established. Fish pieces should be completely immersed in brine and covered with a weight plate. The temperature of the *strong* brine brine should not exceed 60° F (15.5° C). If the brining time exceeds 4 hours, the solution must be placed in a refrigerator 38° F (3° C) or ice should be added to the brine. Adding ice will change the strength of the brine so a better solution is to add re-usable ice packs. Keep in mind that brine loses its strength in time as salt penetrates the meat leaving behind a weaker solution. When brining times are long the solution's strength should be periodically checked with a brine tester and readjusted accordingly.

Most professional literature and practices of commercial plants, Torry Kiln research papers included, choose 80° brine as the over all choice. A 70-80° brine can be employed for all the common types of fish. By placing fish in a strong brine we are performing an all out attack on the bacteria preventing them from growing. Salt penetrates the flesh of fish very rapidly and the brining times are relatively short. Fish brined in 90-100° brine will lose around 3% of its weight.

More uniform salt penetration is obtained when the brining times are longer, but that will require a 30-40 degree solution. In such a brine fish may be left overnight, but will pick up about 2-3% of water which needs to be evaporated during smoking making the process longer.

Making Brine

There isn't a universal brine and every book and recipe provides customized instructions. Many recipes call for mixing salt with water until the egg or potato start to float. We have tried that and the results were misleading. Does anybody think that a fish processing plant will test the brine with an egg or potato?

First, it makes no sense at all to talk about curing time if we don't specify the strength of a brine. We can mix ½ cup salt with one quart of water or we can add 5 cups salt into one gallon of water and it is obvious that curing times will be different though both brines will do the job. To prepare your own brine in a professional way you need two things:

1. Buy a brine tester. They are so cheap that *there is no excuse* for not having one. The salinometer consists of a float with a stem attached, marked in degrees. The instrument will float at its highest level in a saturated brine, and will read 100° degrees (26.4 % salt solution). This is known as a fully saturated brine at 60° F (15.8° C). Beyond this point no more salt can be dissolved in water, the salt will settle down on the bottom of the container. In weaker brines the stem will float at lower levels and the reading will be lower. With no salt present the reading will be 0. To make brine put some water one into a suitable container, add some salt, insert a brine tester and read the scale. Want a stronger solution: add more salt. Need a weaker brine: add more water, it is that simple.

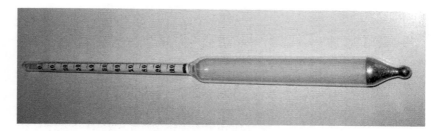

Photo 3.1 Brine tester also known as salinometer or salometer.

Keep in mind that a salinometer's scale measures the density of a solution containing salt and water. Once you add other ingredients they will alter the density of a solution effecting the salinometer reading.

Photo 3.2 Salt is added to water until the correct brine strength is obtained.

Photo 3.3 Brine tester floating in brine.

Photo 3.4 Four gallons of brine that was prepared a day earlier. It is still partially frozen.

Photo 3.5 When mixing ice with water, it is advisable to re-check brine strength with a tester.

The brine tables are tested at 60 F (15.8° C). For other brine temperatures, the observed salinometer readings must be converted before using them. Add one salinometer degree for each 10 degrees above 60° F and subtract one degree for each 10 degrees below 60° F (15.8° C).

2. Making Brine Using Tables - *the fastest way for making brine.*

1. Choose the strength of the brine.
2. Prepare one gallon of water.
3. Weigh the amount of needed salt as listed in the table.
4. Add salt to water, mix and wait to clarify.

Photo 3.6 Weighing salt and measuring one gallon of water.

Photo 3.7 Mixing salt with one gallon of water.

Brine in Salinometer degrees at 60° F	salt (in pounds) to 1 US gal of water	% salt by weight
10	0.22	2.64
20	0.46	5.28
30	0.71	7.91
40	0.98	10.55
50	1.26	13.19
60	1.56	15.83
70	1.88	18.47
80	2.23	21.11
90	2.59	23.75
100	2.98	26.39

To make 80° brine we need to add 2.23 pounds of salt to 1 gallon of water. If you need a smaller quantity of 80° brine, add 1.1 lb salt to half-gallon of water. *The procedure is simple, fast and accurate.* The tables cover brine from 0 - 100° in one degree intervals. There are separate tables for UK gallons (4.54 liter) which can be obtained on the internet.

Complete brine tables are listed in Appendix A.

It does not matter whether US or UK tables are used, as the salt to water ratios remain the same, for example :

	US gallon (3.8 liter)	UK Imperial gallon (4.54 liter)
Salt per gallon	2.22 lb	2.67 lb
% salt by weight	21%	21%
Brine strength	80°	80°

Because UK gallon is bigger, more salt is added, but the percent of salt by weight is the same in UK or US brine of equivalent strength.

Making Small Amounts of Brine

Brine Strength	Salt (in grams) added to *1 quart* of water	Salt (in grams) added to **1 liter** of water	% salt by weight
4°	10 g	11 g	1.0%
10°	24	26	2.6%
20°	50	55	5.2%
30°	79 (1/4 cup)	86	8.0%
40°	105	118	10.5%
50°	145 (1/2 cup)	151	13.2%
60°	178	188	15.8%
70°	214 (3/4 cup)	226	18.4%
80°	248	267	21.0%
90°	294 (1 cup)	311	23.7%
100°	339	358	26.3%

1 liter of water = 1000 g, 1 qt of water = 946 g, 1 cup salt = 292 g,
1 Tablespoon salt = 18 g, 1 teaspoon salt = 6 g, 1 oz = 28.35 g.
1 Tbsp = 3 tsp.
1 US gallon = 3.8 liters = 3.8 kilograms = 8.33 lbs.
Seawater contains approximately 3.695 % salt which corresponds to 14 degrees salometer (°SAL).

Keep in mind that the volume of the brine that was made by combining one gallon of water with 2.2 lbs salt (80° brine) will be larger than one gallon, so use the appropriate container. The main advantage of making your own brine is that you have total control and *there is no guessing involved.*

Baumé Scale

You may come across a popular European Baumé degrees brine scale that is based on the specific gravity of the brine measured with a hydrometer. One can measure the gravity of the brine with a specially designed float (like a brine tester) and one can refer to the table and look up the % NaCl (salt) by weight. One Baumé degree corresponds to 10 g of salt in 1 liter of water. The table below compares SAL brine strength degrees with Baumé scale.

Specific Gravity	% Salt by Weight	Baumé Degrees	Salinometer Degrees
1.007	1	1.0	4
1.014	2	2.0	8
1.022	3	3.1	12
1.029	4	4.1	15
1.037	5	5.2	19
1.044	6	6.1	25
1.051	7	7.0	27
1.058	8	7.9	30
1.066	9	8.9	34
1.073	10	9.8	37
1.081	11	10.9	41
1.089	12	11.9	46
1.096	13	12.7	50
1.104	14	13.7	54
1.112	15	14.6	57
1.119	16	15.4	61
1.127	17	16.3	65
1.135	18	17.2	69
1.143	19	18.1	72
1.151	20	19.0	76
1.159	21	19.9	80
1.168	22	20.9	84
1.176	23	21.7	88
1.184	24	22.5	92
1.192	25	23.4	95
1.201	26	24.3	99

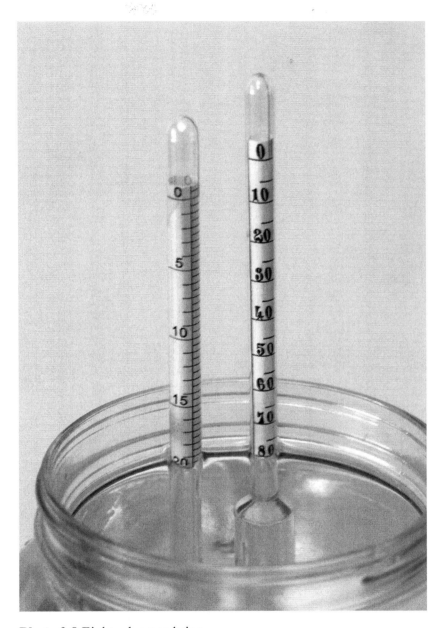

Photo 3.8 Eighty degrees brine.
Left - Baumé hygrometer (20° Be).
Right - Salinometer (80° SAL).
The readings confirm data in the table on the previous page.

Speed of Curing

- The speed of curing depends whether we process whole fish, whole gutted fish, fish steaks or fillets. Fillets with the skin on will cure slower because the skin acts as a barrier that inhibits any flow of solution, moisture or even smoke. The skin with scales will cure even slower.

- At higher temperatures the curing develops faster.

- Fish will cure faster when it receives more salt, whether by dry salting or by being immersed in a heavy brine.

- Fat fish cures slower than the lean ones, reason being that fat inhibits diffusion of salt. Salt dissolves easily in water but not in fat. Lean flesh contains around 80% of water, but fat contains only 10-15% of water.

- Salt penetrates fish easier in places that are open or cut than through the skin.

- Generally speaking, the brining time depends on the size of the fish and the salt concentration of the brine.

It is hard to derive time for fish fillets, fish with the skin on, and little fish or pieces of fish. The fish fillet will be oversalted if immersed for the same time in the same brine as a large fish. When brining fish of different sizes it is advisable to use separate containers and classify fish according to its species and size. When using a single container, place small pieces on top so they can be removed earlier.

Salt penetrates the flesh of the fish within minutes and brining times are much shorter than those for red meats.

"Rule of thumb" brining times for whole fish	
Brine strength in degrees	Brining times in hours
30	10-12
50	3-4
80	1-2

Brining times (80° brine) for *cold smoking:*

½" fillets	-	½ hr
1" fillets	-	1 hr
1 ½" fillets	-	2 hrs

Brining times (80° brine) for *hot smoking:*

½" fillets	-	15 min
1" fillets	-	30 min
1 ½" fillets	-	1 hr
Small whole fish	-	1-3 hours

A medium size herring (fat fish) should remain in 80 degrees brine for about 4 hours. Herring fillets need to be submerged in the same brine for only 20-30 minutes.

For short times the heavy brine can be kept below 60° F (15.8° C). For longer times, the brine should be kept in a cooler.

Fat fish such as salmon, mackerel or herring, should not be exposed to the air when cured, otherwise they may develop brownish spots on the exposed areas and rancidity develops. This is known as "rusting." Keep the fish fully covered with salt or submerged in brine. Commercial producers test brine for microbiological spoilage and can reuse it again, however, in home applications the brine should be changed daily.

Brining and smoking fish is a lot of trial and error and record keeping. Notes should be made for future reference.

A typical 80 degrees brine:

    1 gallon water
    2.25 lbs salt (4 cups)
    1 lb brown sugar
    2 Tbs Cure #1
    1/3 cup lemon juice
    1 Tbs garlic powder
    1 Tbs onion powder
    1 Tbs allspice powder
    1 Tbs white pepper

Photo 3.9 Add ice to brine when weather gets hot.

Photo 3.10 Perch, small trout and 3/8" bluefish fillets were brined for 5 minutes in 80° brine and turned out perfect after smoking.

What's Better Dry Salt or Brine?

It is harder to get consistent results with dry salting as the fish come in different size, weight and shape. The brine, however, *will find a way to enter every little opening.* Brined fish will acquire salt and flavorings in all areas.

If you catch one or two fish, sprinkling with salt may be more practical. It is faster to sprinkle fish with a dry mix and start smoking. It is a question of economics as less space and equipment is required. The processing time is shorter as fish does not need to be dried before the smoke is applied. In addition much salt will be wasted when brine is discarded. There is less salt wasted when sprinkling fish with dry mix.

However, if you process 50 fish, then it becomes a little commercial venture and brining is a better solution. A correct strength brine can be made a day earlier and may be kept in the refrigerator until needed. The advantage of using brine is that once the strength of the brine has been chosen, the product will always be consistent as long as the process time takes into account the size of the fish.

Photo 3.11 Gutted Atlantic mackerel, commercial production.

Photo 3.12 Brining Atlantic mackerel, commercial production.

Smaller establishments such as a fish restaurants or take out stores are very busy and don't have enough storage space to keep fish in tanks. An additional employee might be needed to cope with those additional chores. Brining requires time, the brined fish is wet; it needs to drain and dry out before the smoke can be applied. To save space and time they cure fish with dry mix.

Dry Mixes

Fat fish is often cured with a mixture of salt, sugar and spices. First, the salt is mixed with herbs, spices and flavorings of choice, then the mixture is rubbed gently into the fish. Into the belly, and more on the skin which should be devoid of scales.

General formula for creating your own mix:

Salt, 10-14 g
Sugar, 3-6 g
1.5 g spice mix (pepper, hot pepper, cloves, cinnamon, ginger, nutmeg, mace, bay leaf, mint, hops, etc).

The spices should be finely ground. Crush hops and bay leaves.

Some dry mix combinations:

Ingredients in grams			
	Mix 1	Mix 2	Mix 3
Salt	70	50	75
Sugar	15	10	20
Allspice	2.5	5	2.5
Black pepper	1.0	5	2.5
Red pepper	1.5	0.8	0.5
Cloves	0.8	0.8	1.5
Ginger	0.8	-	1.0
Coriander	0.5	-	-
Nutmeg	0.5	0.8	-
Mace	0.2	-	-
Hops, crushed	-	-	1.0
Cinnamon	-	-	0.5
Bay leaf, crushed	-	-	1.0

The fish is laid down in a container:

- Small fish, less than a pound - 4 hours
- Large fish - 8 hours or overnight

There are many ready to apply dry mixes that can be used for general cooking or smoking fish. Creole Seasoning is an excellent dry mix for smoking fish made by Zatarain's, New Orleans, LA.

Applying Dry Mix

Mix salt with spices of your choice. Rub the mixture all around, inside of the belly included; apply more force and mixture into the skin as the skin slows down salt penetration. The rate of salt penetration is 20% faster in dry-salted fish than in brine. The skin creates obstacles to salt penetration, so this is why the fish skin (not the flesh) is often scorched with a knife. Fillets are very delicate so just sprinkle dry mix on top. Lay the fish flat in a container and place in refrigerator.

Rinse the fish briefly with tap water and proceed to smoking.

Note: dry salting fillets will result in drawing out the mixture of water, blood and proteins to the surface. If the split fish or a fillets are lying flat on screens, little liquid paddles will form which will become white curd during smoking and cooking. This is a smaller problem in fish that are secured by hanging as this protein solution will drip down.

Small fish	*Fillets*		
3/4 lb - 3 hours salting time.	½" fillets	-	10 min
1 lb - 3 hours	1" fillets	-	25 min
	1 ½" fillets	-	45 min

More About Salt

For brining purposes both table salt and kosher salt will work equally well in terms of providing the desired effects, though kosher salt, particularly Diamond® Crystal kosher salt dissolves more readily. What is important to remember is that kosher salts are less dense than ordinary table salts and measure quite differently from a volume standpoint. Kosher salt has larger crystals and is bulkier. For example a given weight of Diamond® Crystal takes up nearly twice the volume as the same weight of table salt. Non-iodized salt should be used, canning rock salt is a good choice.

Table salt	1 cup	292 g (10.3 oz)
Morton® Kosher Salt	1-1/3 to 1-1/2 cup	218 g (7.7 oz)
Diamond® Crystal Kosher Salt	2 cups	142 g (5 oz)

As you can see *it is always advisable to weigh out your salt.*

Adding Spices to Brine

For an extra flavor, spices can be added, however add them to weak brines only. Strong brines, 70-90°, do not leave enough time for the spices to bring any significant effect. About 1 tablespoon of herbs (spices) spices can be added to one gallon of brine. Use ingredients that you like most, after all you will eat the fish. Some of the popular seasonings: pepper, parsley, dill, capers, mustard seeds, rosemary, juniper, onion, cilantro, bay leaf, celery leaves, sugar, vinegar, lemon juice. You can try commercially produced seasonings which are sold in stores.

After brining, briefly wash fish to eliminate excess salt and any traces of blood. Drain the fish, place them on screens or hang them and let dry. Then proceed to smoking.

Brine Marinades

Sugar, herbs and spices may be added to brine to produce original flavor. To saturate fish with customized flavors, the fish has to remain in brine for longer period of time, preferably overnight. Heavy brine such as 80° is not suitable as the fish will be over salted. A very lightly salted brine is needed which may as well be called the brine marinade. Keep in mind that such a weak solution cannot be used in fish that will be cold smoked.

Four degrees brine is a good all around salt solution that needs only herbs and flavorings to become the marinade.

4° brine- add 10 g (1-1/2 tsp) salt to 1 quart of water.

About 1-2 tablespoon of flavor inducing ingredients are added to two gallons of 4° brine.

Popular ingredients are: dill, parsley, sage, thyme, capers, basil, rosemary, juniper berries, mustard seeds, garlic, ginger, onion, peppers, sugar, lemon juice, soy sauce, Worcestershire sauce and vinegar.

The marinade should have the dominant flavor; this would be the herb or spice that you like most. Such an herb can be inserted into the fish the moment the fish has been gutted and washed in order to imparts its flavor to the fish. Then, the fish should be fully immersed in marinade overnight.

Brining Fish

If you decide to use a strong brine, the whole process of smoking fish can be accomplished in 3-4 hours. You can, however, place fish in a weak brine, leave them overnight (10-12 hours) in refrigerator and start smoking the next day. Chicken is marinated the same way although fish brine is weaker. It is recommended to start with with a weak brine and keep notes for reference. There is not much we can do to over salted fish.

Making Small Amount of Brine

Brine Strength	Water	Salt	%salt
4°	1 qt	10 g	1%
10°	1 qt	24 g	2.6%
20°	1 qt	50 g	5.2%
30°	1 qt	79 g	8%
40°	1 qt	105 g	10%
80°	1 qt	248 g	21%
1 cup salt = 292 g, 1 Tablespoon salt = 18 g, 1 teaspoon salt = 6 g * For making small amount of brine in liters, see Appendix.			

Curing times for small fish and fillets:

Fish	Salt	Water	% salt	Brine	Time
Small fish	10 g	1 qt	1%	4°	10-12 hrs
Small fish	24 g	1 qt	2.6%	10°	2 hours
Fillets, 1/2-1"	24 g	1 qt	2.6%	10°	30-45 min
1 teaspoon of common table salt weighs 6 g.					

Brine temperature should be kept about 50° F (10° C); below this temperature the rate of salt uptake is reduced.

Photo 3.13 Smoked fish.

Chapter 4

Conditioning Fish

The characteristic flavor of the fish is mainly due to salt and smoke, but the texture and color of its flesh is greatly influenced by drying the fish prior to smoking. Weaker brines or not salting fish at all leaves smoked fish with a rather dull appearance. After brining the fish are carefully rinsed under cold running water to remove salt crystals and any traces of spices from the surface. Letting them to drain for 10-15 minutes will shorten drying.

Photo 4.1 Draining fish.

Before smoke is applied the surface of the fish must be dry or feel at least "tacky" to touch for the proper development of color. Wet surface may attract smoke, but it will also attract undesirable elements of smoke such as soot and other not fully burnt particles. This will darken the surface and create less attractive color.

Photo 4.2 Wet fish are drying until they feel dry or at least tacky to touch. No smoke is applied yet.

There are two types of drying:

Low temperature drying. The purpose is to remove moisture from the surface of the fish. The cleaned fish are placed in a draughty area (fan works well) until they feel dry to touch. The fish can be dried in a smokehouse at 85-100° F (30-38° C). The purpose of this type of drying is to prepare fish for hot smoking and to develop skin gloss. Little fish and fillets will be processed this way. The smoke can be applied when the fish feel dry or tacky to touch.

High temperature drying. The purpose is to firm up the fish and harden the skin, so its head will not break away from the body during smoking. This is important when *large* whole fish are hung during smoking. The fish may start drying at 100° F (38° C), but the temperature increases gradually to 158° F (70° C). The smoke may be applied at this stage.

Photo 4.3 Fish may be patted dry with a paper towel, then left briefly to dry. If insects are present, the fish should be dried out in a pre-heated snokehouse.

Ideally, drying should be performed without smoke. This is easy to accomplish when the smokehouse runs on electricity or gas. When wood is the heating medium, the logs should be pre-burned first and then added to the fire pit. A thin smoke is acceptable.

Drying can be performed at 100° F (43° C) or higher. The smokehouse should be preheated first. Russian and Polish commercial producers dry fish at 140-158° F (60-70° C). Drying at these temperatures starts destroying bacteria. Make note that drying at those temperatures will cook surface proteins and cannot be applied to cold smoking method. Drying toughens the fish so there is less possibility it will break at the head. The fish will continue to dry when hot smoke is applied. Keep in mind, the drying of the fish will be impaired if performed at 75% humidity or higher. All dampers should be open to create the maximum draft (flow of air) and to facilitate removal of moisture.

Pellicle

Most smoked products are not eaten immediately after cooking, but later. They must look presentable and appealing to a customer. Smoked fish should have a glossy appearance, it should shine. This shine known as "pellicle" is due to the reaction between salt and fish proteins. Salt "swells" the proteins and they unwind and release some of their contents. Some of those proteins dissolve in salt and become a sticky substance (exudate) that travels to the surface of the fish. After drying this sticky substance becomes a shiny protein coat known as *"pellicle"* that may be compared to shoe polish. After smoking this clear *pellicle* becomes a shiny lacquer on the surface of the fish. The longer the brined fish are allowed to hang, within reason, the better the gloss that develops. *The best gloss develops with 70-80° brine.* To develop pellicle one hour is probably the minimum, but for a large fish 12 hours or more is not uncommon. Previously frozen fish produces very little *pellicle.* If dry salt is applied with pepper and other spices, this gloss will be less noticeable as the spices will remain on the surface.

Photo 4.4 Atlantic mackerel waiting for the smokehouse.

Photo 4.5 The fish in lower right corner was sprinkled with dry mix. It has none of the shine of the fish that was salted or brined with salt alone.

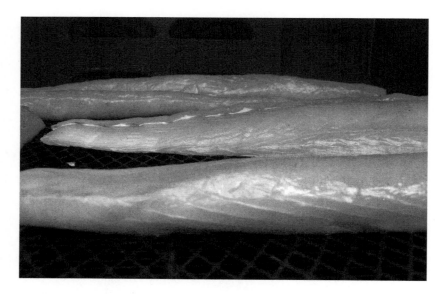

Photo 4.6 Well developed pellicle in Spanish mackerel fillet.

Photo 4.7 Pellicle in smoked fish fillet. The unsmoked fish fillet (top photo) has a greyish shine and the smoked one exhibits a golden gloss.

Photo 4.8 Drying Atlantic mackerel before smoking.

Photo 4.9 Smoked Atlantic mackerel.

The flesh of fish is delicate by nature and they have to be handled gently when hanging them. When hanging fillets it is advisable to leave the skin on otherwise the fillets may break apart.

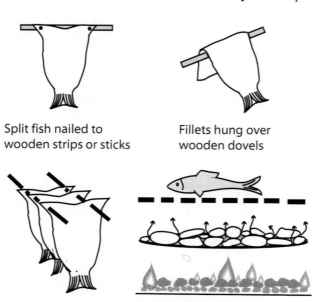

Split fish nailed to
wooden strips or sticks

Fillets hung over
wooden dovels

Split fish hung on dovels

Whole fish or fillets may
be placed on screen

Fig. 4.1 Hanging fillets.

Fig. 4. 2 Reinforcing fish
with butcher twine.

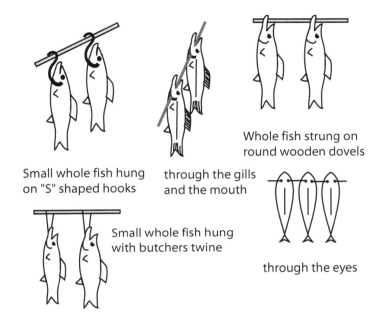

Small whole fish hung on "S" shaped hooks

through the gills and the mouth

Whole fish strung on round wooden dovels

Small whole fish hung with butchers twine

through the eyes

Fig. 4.3 Hanging small fish.

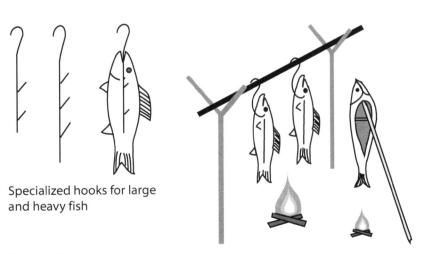

Specialized hooks for large and heavy fish

Fig. 4.4 Hanging large fish.

Fig. 4.5 Smoking over camp fire.

The main difficulty has been that when the split fish such as kippers (split herring) or butterflied mullet are left to drip on trays, a small pool of brine remains in the belly cavity of the fish; this leaves either a wet patch on the fish after smoking or, if the pool dries up, a white curd substance which spoils the appearance of the product. It is possible, however, to overcome this problem by draining the split fish at the angle or by placing them flesh side down.

Specialty Hooks

The beheaded or split belly open fish may be hung with a twine loop or by using a specialty hook. Such a hook may be made from stainless steel wire or wire hanger. This arrangement will prevent fat from dripping down.

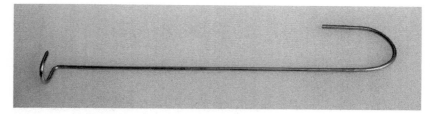

Photo 4.10 A fish hanging hook.

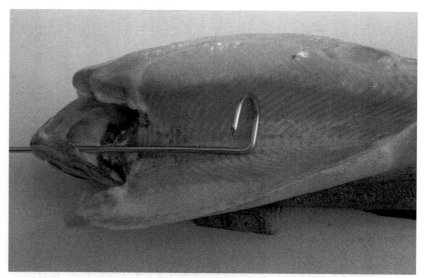

Photo 4.11 The hook can be used on a headed or beheaded fish.

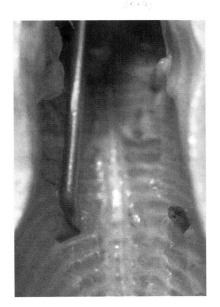

Photo 4.12 The hook goes behind the spine.

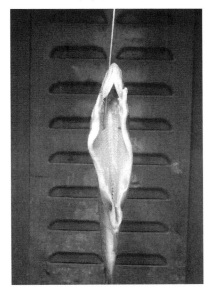

Photo 4.13 Secured fish.

Photo 4.14 A stick and twine.

Photo 4.15 Stainless steel clip.

Hardening the Fish

Whole *heavy* fish breaks free sometimes at the head when being smoked. This is often attributed to the high temperature of smoking, however, the high humidity is the factor that compounds the problem. When the fish is inserted on a smokestick through the eyes, a support is created in which the head holds the body. However, there are very few muscles inside the head, just a small amount of connective tissue. The skin contains plenty of connective tissue which like head contains collagen. This tissue will harden in time and become stronger, but the drying significantly slows down at high humidity. As a result, the heat builds up inside the head and the connective tissue softens and melts into gel. The head collapses.

This usually occurs only when the humidity is very high and at the beginning of drying or smoking. The solution is to dry the fish at low temperatures 95-104° F (35-40° C) when the humidity is 80-100%. When humidity is at 50-60%, the drying can proceed at 140-158° F (60-70° C). Generally speaking, to increase the the mechanical strength of fish, the temperatures during drying and smoking should be increased gradually. The fish will hold its shape better, the flesh will have a firmer texture and the skin will not separate from the flesh.

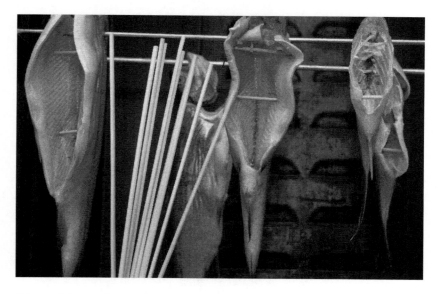

Photo 4.16 A piece of wooden skewer or even toothpick will keep the belly from closing during smoking.

Chapter 5

Smoking Fish

Salting and smoking fish was practiced for centuries. Man discovered that smoking was a very effective tool in preserving fish. Heavy salting and long periods of cold smoking preserved fish well enough so they could be kept for months without spoiling. Since Middle Ages until 1900's fish were heavily cured with salt and *cold smoked* for 3 weeks or more. With the development of railways (1840), it became possible to distribute fresh fish to wider areas and the fishing industry started to grow rapidly. Due to the availability of fresh fish, the taste for heavily salted, smoked and dried fish has declined, and people came to prefer less salty foods. Fish are hot smoked today for a pleasant taste what is achieved with less salt and shorter smoking times. Refrigeration takes care of preserving foods.

Beside enhancing the taste and look, smoking increases the product's shelf life. It helps preserve the meat by slowing down the spoilage of fat and growth of bacteria. The advantages of smoking fish are numerous:

- Slows down the growth of bacteria.
- Prevents fats from developing a rancid taste.
- Extends the shelf life of the product.
- Develops a new taste and flavor.
- Changes the color, smoked products shine and look better.

The main reason to smoke fish at home today is to produce a product that cannot be obtained in a typical store. One can order traditionally made products on the Internet but they will be very expensive.

What is Smoking ?

Smoking meat is exactly what the name implies: flavoring meat with smoke. Using any kind of improvised device will do the job as long as smoke contacts the meat surface. The strength of the flavor depends mainly on the time and density of the smoke. Smoke is a mixture of air and gases created during wood combustion. What we see is a stream of gases such as nitrogen, carbon dioxide, carbon monoxide, water vapor, and sulphur dioxide that carry unburned particles such as tar, resins, soot and air borne ash. The actual composition of the smoke depends on the type of wood, its moisture content, combustion temperature, and the amount of available air. It is estimated that smoke consists of about 10,000 individual components and a few hundred of these are responsible for the development of a smoky flavor.

The air draft, which might be considered the smokehouse sucking power, sucks in the outside air and combustion gases that in turn attract solid unburned particles such as soot, ash and others. This stream rushes inside of the smoking chamber where it collides with hanging meats and with the walls of the chamber. A stronger air draft and higher temperature increase the energy of the smoke which results in more intense smoking. The amount of moisture on the surface of a product plays a role in color formation and the color develops faster when the surface is wetter. This also results in a much darker color as particles such as tar and soot easily stick to the surface.

Smoking meat consists of the following steps:

- Curing with salt
- Applying smoke
- Cooking

Meat can be smoked yet still be raw inside. It must be cooked to proper temperature before it is ready to consume. This cooking process may be accomplished in a smokehouse or in an oven. Some products are smoked at low temperatures and never cooked. The safety of these products is obtained by heavy salting and removal of moisture. Such products are cold smoked.

There are two methods of smoking:

1. Cold smoking, at temperatures below 85° F (30° C).

2. Hot smoking, at temperatures from 140-284° F (60-140° C).

Many people assume that each method uses rigidly implemented range of temperatures and processing times, but this is not true, especially for the hot smoking method.

Smoking methods	Cold	Hot
Time required	days, weeks	hours
Temperature	below 85° F (30° C)	120-220° F (50-104° C)
Salt needed	Yes, a large amount	little, just for flavor
Method of preserving (killing bacteria)	salt plus *drying* to remove moisture	high temperature to kill bacteria
Product shelf life	long	short
Texture	firm	soft
Taste	good	very good
Curing	prolonged heavy salting	of little significance
Cooking	none	yes
Smoke penetration	In all areas of meat	Surface areas only.

After smoking the fish will weigh less due to the loss of moisture. The yield of the *hot smoked fish* is about 70-75% in relation to the weight of the fish before drying. The yield of the *cold smoked fish* is about 55-60% in relation to the weight of the fish before drying. The majority of fish is hot smoked today as preserving them is accomplished in a refrigerator. Canning takes care of fish products that need to be stored for a long time without refrigeration.

Cold Smoking Fish

Cold smoking is an old technique that was practiced not because it produced great flavor, but because it helped to preserve meats. There was no refrigeration, but meats had to be preserved. *Cold smoking is drying meat with smoke.* Its purpose is elimination of moisture so that bacteria would not grow. This technique developed in North European countries where the climate was harsh and winters severe. When meats were cold smoked for 2-3 weeks, yes, the meat became preserved due to the loss of moisture, but *it was drying that made the meat safe.* If the same meat was dried at 54° F (12° C) *without* smoke, it would be preserved all the same. Fish is smoked below 80° F (26° C) from 1-5 days. Temperatures above 80° F (26° C) will cook the fish. Cold smoked fish is considered raw meat as it is never exposed to high temperatures. That is why it has to be heavily salted or brined at 16% salt (65 degrees brine or higher) to provide safety to the consumer. The best range of humidity for cold smoking at 80-85° F is 60-70%.

There is no cooking. The longer the smoking period the more moisture is removed, the drier the product becomes, and of course it develops a longer shelf life. This method of smoking can last up to a few weeks and the fish will have excellent keeping qualities. After prolonged cold smoking the fish has lost enough moisture to be considered safe without cooking. Fish that were cold smoked hold well together and can be very finely sliced which cannot be done if the fish were hot smoked. Traditionally made cold smoked products contained up to 15% salt and were smoked and dried for a long time.

Cold smoking is not a continuous process, it is stopped (no smoke) a few times to allow fresh air into the smoker. Because of the time and costs involved the cold smoking is rarely used today. In addition, cold smoked products are heavily salted which makes them less appealing to a health conscious consumer of today. The majority of hobbyists think of cold smoking as some mysterious preservation technique that will produce a unique and superb quality product. *Cold smoking is not a preservation method, it will not preserve meat unless proper conditions are established for the meat to dry.*

Photo 5.1 Cold smoking at its best. Waldemar Kozik is making meat products of the highest quality at the Catskill Mountains of New York.

Photo 5.2 Cold smoking is still practiced today. Waldemar Kozik cold smoking Hungarian salami. There is no room for chemicals, binders or colorants here, just quality meats, Mother Nature and the art of smoking of Mr. Waldemar. The same way it has been done for centuries, the right way.

Photo 5.3 Fresh fish.   **Photo 5.4** Smoked fillets.

The pigs were traditionally slaughtered for Christmas and the meat had to last until the summer. Noble cuts were cooked or salted, the trimmings were used for sausages. They needed to be dried to last through the winter. That was not easy with freezing temperatures outside. The only way to heat up storage facilities was to burn the wood that produced the smoke. There were two choices for protecting meats from the heat:

- Hanging meats 5 feet above a small smoldering fire *OR*
- Burning wood in a firebox that was located outside. The firebox was connected with the smokehouse by an underground channel that would supply heat and smoke at the same time.

A large smokehouse was also a storage facility; after meat was smoked, it was hung in a different area where it continued to receive some smoke, although on a much smaller scale.

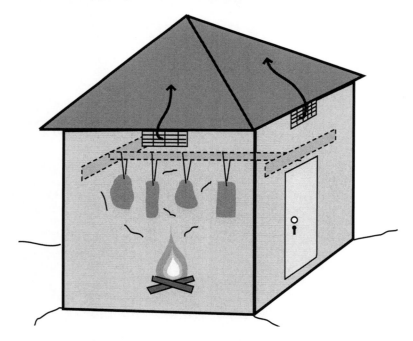

Fig. 5.1 American style colonial smokehouse.

This prevented molds from growing, as molds need oxygen to live. It had been established that meats dried best when the temperatures were somewhere between 50 – 60° F (10 - 15° C) and although the temperature of the smoke leaving the firebox was higher, it would be just right by the time it made contact with meat. Whole logs of wood were burnt, wood shavings and sawdust were used to control the fire. The fire was allowed to die out as people went to sleep. The meats hung through the night and the fire was re-started again. So, when you see an old recipe saying that ham or sausage was smoked for 2 weeks, well, it really was not, as it probably received continuous smoke for about 1/2 of the time.

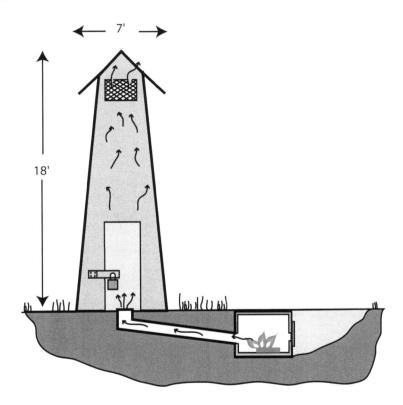

Fig. 5.2 Lithuanian smokehouse with an outside smoke generator.

Those meats were not cooked, they were dried and could be considered fermented products. There is little difference about Italian salami, Hungarian salami or Polish Cold Smoked Sausage.

Italian salami was dried without smoke and Hungarian salami or Polish sausage were dried with cold smoke. Italians and Spaniards were blessed with a climate that provided cool prevailing winds at right temperatures. *There was no need to burn wood to warm up the drying chambers.* As a result products did not acquire smoky flavor. For this reason people in Mediterranean basin are not particularly fond of smoked products, and people in Germany, Poland, Russia, Lithuania love them, but don't generally like uncooked air dried products. The majority of all processed meat products in Northern Europe are of smoked variety.

All Polish, German, Russian or Lithuanian technology books about smoking agree that cold smoke should be applied below 72° F (22° C). Occasionally a book calls for 77° F (25° C). Old German books specify temperature of cold smoke as 64° F (18° C) or lower. Any recipe that calls for cold smoke higher than 85° F (30° C) makes little sense, as *at this temperature proteins coagulate and the texture of the meat changes.* The meat gets cooked. The surface area will harden preventing moisture removal and the product will rot inside. This hardened ring will also slow down smoke penetration.

To summarize, the purpose of cold smoking was to dry meats. *The product was drying out and the smoke happened to be there.* Preservation was on people's mind and not creating cold smoked flavor.

Early Commercial Fish Smokehouses

Meats and sausages were smoked by butchers in small smokehouses. Small smokehouses could hardly cope with the demand of the fishing industry. First industrial type smokehouses appeared in England and were specifically dedicated to smoking fish. Since electricity was not invented yet, the units were designed for cold smoking. Often entire buildings were converted into smokehouses, where the basement served as the smoke generator and the fish were placed on the first, 2nd or 3rd level.

Unit A - first generation multi-chamber smokehouse

Individual smokehouses were constructed on both sides of the chimney. That was a rather inefficient design as it required heating up not only each of the units (A) but the entire smokehouse chamber as well. Needless to say the wood usage was huge. The exiting smoke was controlled by a common to all chimney damper (5).

Unit B - improved design

A metal plate (1) was placed on top of each unit. This metal ceiling had an adjustable opening that was controlled by a flat metal damper (2). The weakness of this design was moisture gathered in the corners under the ceiling (p) which was dripping down on hanging products decreasing their looks and quality. The chimney damper was not needed anymore.

Unit C - second generation multi-chamber smokehouse

The next improvement was a design where each unit was independent of the others. It had a steep sloping conical ceiling (3) that provided an easier exit path for the smoke eliminating the problem of moisture pockets. The top of the ceiling was covered by an adjustable metal plate (4) that was controlled by a pull chain.

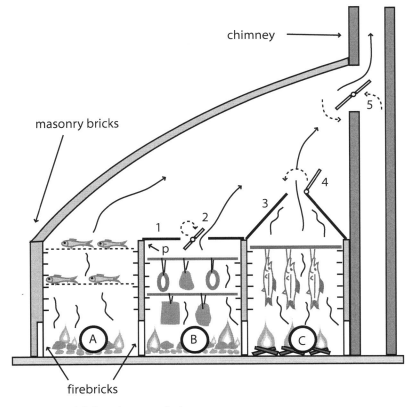

Fig. 5.3 Multichamber smokehouse.

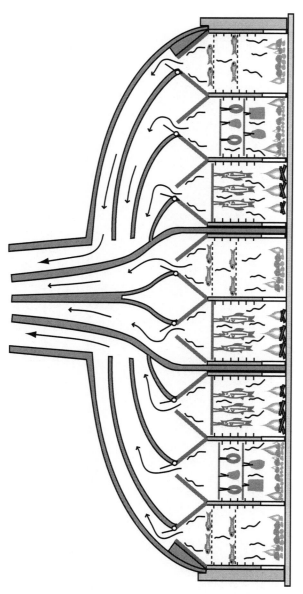

Fig. 5.4 Improved design multichamber smokehouse.

A few units shared a common exit channels that led into a common chimney. Some units were dedicated to cold smoking and some to hot smoking as the areas were physically separated. In some smokehouses each unit had its own exit channel that would enter a shared chimney.

Multilevel Smokehouses

Many three story buildings were converted into commercial smokehouses for smoking fish.

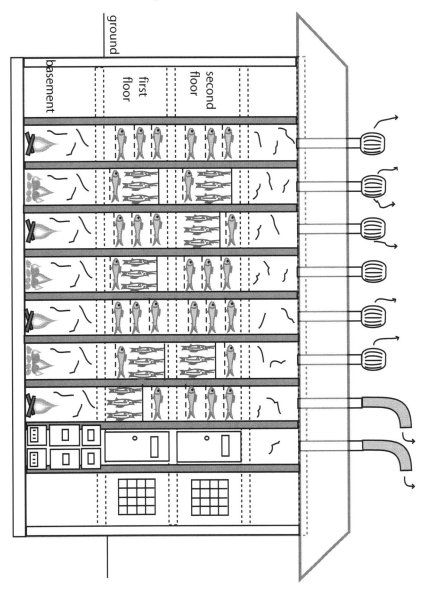

Fig. 5.5 Multilevel smokehouse.

A typical smokehouse would consist of:

- Basement-where a firebox/smoke producer would be located.
- First floor- smoke chamber.
- Second floor-smoke chamber.

There were 3-10 individual smoke chambers. They were divided by a brick wall going all the way from the basement to the roof. The smoke would exit through an adjustable hinged door or through rotating wind turbines. The units were about 3'6" wide and up to 15 feet long. The width was more critical as the worker was using corbels that protruded from the wall as a ladder. He was climbing up them to hang the smoke sticks that were passed to him from another worker standing below. On each wall there were about 20 corbels separated from each other by about 5 inches. Each unit on the second floor had its own door that gave access to the smoke chamber. After opening the door a wooden board was placed on top of the beams to provide a walkway for hanging more fish inside.

As technology evolved, the brick and cinder block smokehouses were replaced with insulated stainless steel units. Electrical blowers and metal ducts were supplying smoke and the rotating dampers distributed heat precisely to all areas of the smokehouse. This second generation of smokehouses was called the batch oven type. In batch smokehouses, the meat is hung on smoke sticks or placed on stationary racks for the entire smoking process. Then came smokehouses where meat traveled through the various zones (smoking, heating, chilling) within the smokehouse. The product was packaged and stored or shipped.

Hot smoked products traditional in the UK probably originated in Germany and Holland, where mainly fatty fish were processed in small brick kilns capable of reaching a high temperature and retaining the heat; hardwood logs damped with wet sawdust gave a lot of heat and intense smoke. The heat and humidity gave a cooked product that had a golden brown color and a silky sheen on the skin.

Torry Kiln Smokehouse

Until 1939 most smokehouses were always built the same. They depended on a natural draft movement (air going up) to control the flow of heat and smoke without any means of humidity control. The majority of these smokehouses smoked meats for preservation purposes and the temperature was of little concern as long as the smoke was cold.

Torry Kiln was the first design that employed an independent means of draft and temperature control. It was a mechanical kiln that used blowers to push smoke and electrical or steam heaters to generate heat. The Torry Kiln design allowed for precise control of smoking parameters such as air temperature, its speed, and humidity. As a result the finished product was always of a consistent high quality. The Torry Kiln design incorporated a motor-driven fan, electric heaters, temperature sensors, air-diffusers, and even a photo-electric eye for smoke density control.

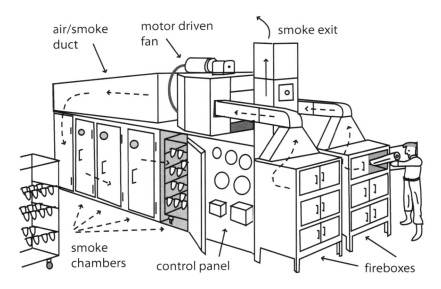

Fig. 5.6 Torry Kiln smokehouse.

The inlet and outlet diffuser walls allowed for a very uniform air flow in all areas of the smokehouse. At the bottom part of the channel there was a recirculation damper (12) that controlled how much air was going out to the chimney (13) and how much air was returning back towards the fan (5). Fresh air was brought into the same area (14). Temperature sensors (15) controlled heaters (4 and 10).

Smoke was generated by three independently controlled fireboxes (1) that were standing above each other. Each had its own loading door and smoke damper. That provided a large smoke generating area without taking up much space. It also prevented soot and other large unburned particles from reaching hanging fish. The smoke would enter a common duct (2) and would be deflected by aerofoils (3) towards the electric heater (4). The motor-driven fan (5) would blow the heated air through the adjustable vertical blinds (6) towards aerofoil plates (7). At the bottom of the diffuser channel the air had to pass through the inlet diffuser wall (8) that contained many individually adjustable openings for the air flow adjustment. From there the heated air or smoke would pass through loaded with fish trolleys (9). Inside the smoke chamber there was an additional booster electric heater (10). The air/smoke leaving the chamber had to pass through the outlet diffuser wall (11) that consisted of fully adjustable openings.

The Torry kiln, designed originally for cold smoking, has been successfully adapted to hot smoking by provision of additional heaters and improved smoke producers, so that most traditional products can be reproduced with adequate color and uniform weight loss. Full details of construction and operation are given in 'Fish Smoking: A Torry Kiln Operator's Hndbook'.

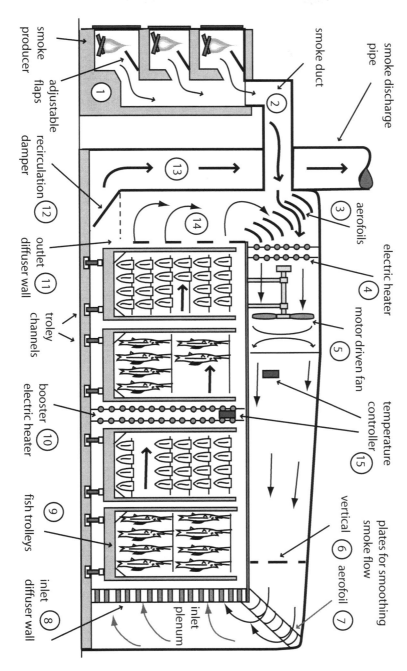

Fig. 5.7 Torry Kiln cross-section view.

Torry Kiln Fish Smoking Times

Torry Kiln is a very efficient smokehouse where smoke parameters, humidity and air velocity are precisely controlled. For a home made smokehouse, smoking times should be increased.

Fish Type	Smoking time in hours (temperature-below 85° F, 30° C)	Soaking time in 80° brine
*Finnan haddocks <1 lb	3	7 min
*Finnan haddocks 1-1-1/4 lb	4	10 min
*Finnan haddocks >1-1-1/4 lb	6	15 min
*Glasgow pales	2 - 2.5	4-5 min
Cod and haddock fillets	2 - 5	4 - 10 min
*Golden cutlets	2 - 3	4 min
**Kippers	4	15 min
**Kipper fillets	2.5-3	3-4 min
**Bloaters	4	dry salt, 8 hrs
Salmon fillet 1.5-2 lb	12	dry salt, 12 hrs
Salmon fillet 3-4 lb	12	dry salt, 16-20 hrs
Salmon fillet 5 lb	12	dry salt, 24 hrs
Cod roe	6-8 hrs, 90-100° F	dry salt, 6-8 hrs
**Buckling	3 hrs, 80-120-170° F	60 min
Smokies 0.5-0.75 lb	3 hrs, 80-120-170° F	30-45 min
Trout	2.5 hrs, 90-180° F	60 min
Sprats	1	15 min
*Seelachs fillets, thin	30 min	dry salt, 12 hrs
*Seelachs fillets, medium	30 min	dry salt, 16-20 hrs
*Seelachs fillets, thick	45 min	dry salt, 24 hrs
Smoked oysters	30 min at 180° F	5 min in 50° brine

* cod family
** herring family

Seelachs include Cowley and Saithe.

Smokehouses for Cold Smoking

The variety of smokers are amazing and each owner swears by his own as doing the best job. Fish smokes and cooks much faster than meat or sausages so the technical expectations from a smoker are a bit lower. *A **smokehouse is just a tool** but smoking is time, temperature, and humidity, and how you control those parameters.* The tool does not make a quality product - YOU DO! *If you understand the smoking process you will create a top quality product in any smoker and in any conditions.*

Any enclosure that will hold smoke and heat can be considered a smoker and will do a good job. To illustrate our point look at the stump smoker below. Most unusual but effective smoker made from the stump of an old oak tree. This original set up has been in operation for 20 years. Smoker located on Poliwoda Fishing Grounds, Opole, Poland. Smoked trout ends up on a dinner plate in a popular tourist restaurant which is located on the same grounds.

Photo 5.5 Brined fish being inserted on smokesticks.

Photo 5.6 A separate fire pit burning wood logs can be seen in the photo in the front.
A sheet of metal covers the smoke delivery channel and the bricks lying on top provide stability. It is connected with a smoker by an underground pipe. On the right of the smoker is a black old potato burlap bag that is used as the smoker's cover. Note that a potato burlap sack makes an excellent cover allowing just the right amount of smoke to slip through.

Photo 5.7 Preparing trout for smoking.

There is less expectation from a smoker which is dedicated for cold smoking only. A cold smoking unit has no need for high temperatures and that is why its design is so simple. The outside conditions are a deciding factor whether cold smoke can be produced. In many areas you cannot produce cold smoke in the summer, unless the steps are taken to cool it. You can produce cold smoke in tropical regions in winter months at night time, but keep in mind that the humidity will be high. Humidity meters are inexpensive so get one. Any enclosure such as carton box, drum barrel, wooden box is suitable as long as the flames will not make direct contact with fish. The traditional solution is to have a free standing fire pit which is connected to the smoking box by a pipe or underground channel.

Smokers that are capable of cold smoking are usually large units as the smoke generating section (firebox) must be located in a safe distance from the fish. It could be located at the bottom of the smoking chamber as long as one or more safety baffles are installed in between. If not, the dripping fat will start the fire. The best solution is to have a free standing firebox, but that makes the unit even bigger.

Photo 5.8 Firebox connected to a smoking chamber by the pipe. The interior volume of the smoking chamber is 20 cubic feet.

Photo 5.9 The same unit, with   **Photo 5.10** Side view.
the flexible dryer pipe. Back
view.

Concrete Block Smoker

An excellent smoker can be built without any tools in a matter of
hours by using standard 8" x 8" x 16" concrete blocks.

Photo 5.11 Concrete block smoker.
  The plans and the detailed description are in Appendix A.

Hot Smoking Fish

During hot smoking the product is smoked and cooked at the same time making it ready to eat. For hot smoking the smokehouse temperature may vary from 120°-284° F (50-140° C) or even higher. Those upper temperatures are nothing else than barbecuing fish. Hot smoking contributes to the safety of the product, however, this beneficial effect is confined to the surface of the fish. The safety is achieve by killing bacteria with heat. The 2-3% salt in present day smoked products is too low to prevent spoilage and they have to be kept in refrigerator. Hot smoking involves the following steps:

- Curing with salt
- Drying
- Smoking/Cooking

Hot smoking is basically performed in three stages:

1. A preliminary drying period at 86° F (30° C) during which the skin is hardened to prevent breakage. The air dampers are fully open for maximum air flow and moisture removal. This period lasts from 30-60 minutes.

2. A heavy smoke is applied for about 30-45 minutes with the exit smoke damper left at ¼ open position. The temperature is gradually raised to 122° F (50° C).

3. The temperature is raised to 176-180° F (80-82° C) and the fish is cooked to 145° F (63° C) internal temperature for a minimum of 30 minutes. Depending on the size of the fish this stage may last from 30–60 minutes. A light smoke may be maintained. When the temperature is raised to 176-180° F (80-82°C) the fish is cooked. Fish is considered done when cooked to 145° F (63° C) internal temperature. Typical fish fillets are smoked from 1 to 5 hours depending on the size. When smoking is finished, the fish should be first air cooled to the ambient temperature and then kept under refrigeration to prevent the growth of microorganisms. This cooling process should be accomplished within 12 hours. The moisture content of most smoked fish averages 60-75% which is still much too high to inhibit growth of bacteria so the fish have to be kept under refrigeration. Fish is cooked when its meat flakes out easily when pressed with a knife or a fork.

Different sources quote different temperatures and processing times so use your own judgement.

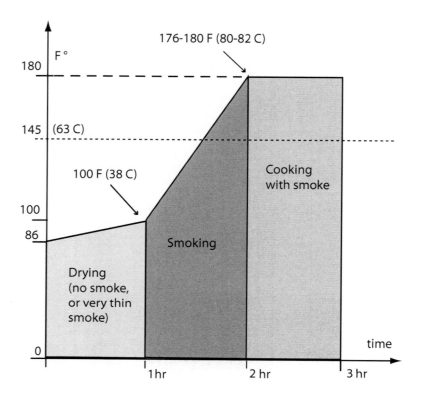

Fig. 5.8 A typical hot smoking of the fish.

The parameter that overrides all others is the safety of the product; the internal meat temperature as recommended by our government - the fish should be cooked to 145° F and held at this temperature for 30 minutes. Once, this temperature is reached the product is safe to consume. It makes little difference whether the fish was processed at 70, 80° C or 100° C, as long as the 145° F (63° C) requirement was met. It will turn out to be fine at all three settings, of course, the length of processing time will be different at each temperature setting. The control of brining, drying and smoking factors is left to the discretion of the person conducting those operations. In time you will be able to use your own judgement and the cause of action taken will be based on factors such as the type and the fattiness of the fish, its size and how it was prepared (whole fish, split fish or fillets). Those factors will influence processing parameters, however, the safe cooking temperature is constant, the fish is either cooked on not.

Cold smoked products are exception as their safety does not depend on heat, but on the amount of lost moisture. In most home made smokers the internal meat temperature lags the smokehouse temperature by about 25-30 degrees. For example, to reach 180° F (82° C) internal fish temperature the smokehouse must be capable to maintain from 200° F (104° C) to 225° F (108° C). In winter, it may be difficult task for a metal barrel smoker to accomplish, unless it is heavily insulated. If the smoker cannot reach required temperature, the fish can be smoked long enough to acquire the color and the flavor, but *the cooking step can be completed in an oven.*

Hot Smoking Fish In Russia and Poland

Both countries are known for producing excellent smoked hams and sausages. During communist era Poland has been building not only fish trawlers but the mother factory ships that were receiving fish catches from fishing trawlers. The factory ship would collect fish from fishing trawlers and process and can fish at sea. Russia produces a large assortment of seafood products and accounts for 95% production of caviar. To make it short both countries were established players in the fish processing field. While writing this book we studied many Polish and Russian technology books on the subject of fish processing. What we have found is that both countries, as well as Germany, smoke fish at high temperatures.

Country	Fish Smoking Method	Temperature
England	Cold	60-86° F (15-30° C)
	Hot	up to 212° F (100° C)
Germany	Hot	212-284° F (100-140° C)
Poland	Cold	68-82° F (20-28° C)
	Hot	158-284° F (70-140° C)
Russia	Cold	68-90° F (20-32° C)
	Hot	176-248° F (80-120°)
		Data from 1960

The smoking process consists of three steps:

1. Drying
2. Cooking
3. Smoking

Drying. The main purpose of drying is to remove moisture and harden the skin and head. As a result the skin does not crack during the second smoking stage which takes place at higher temperature. The head also hardens and will not break away later. Keep in mind that a large fish is heavy but the flesh is quite delicate. The smokehouse is preheated with wood chunks, then the fish is placed inside. All dampers are open to facilitate removal of moisture. The drying takes place at 140-176° F (60-80° C) and continues for 30-60 minutes.

Cooking. More wood chips are added and the temperature is gradually raised. The fish is baked at 230-284° (110-140 C). Wood chips are burned with small flame. The exit damper is gradually decreased, sawdust is added on hot coals, and thicker smoke is produced.

Note: fat fish should be cooked at temperatures not exceeding 212° F (100° C), otherwise the fat will start dripping down.

Smoking. The smoking continues, but the temperature is allowed to slowly drop down below 230° F (110° C).

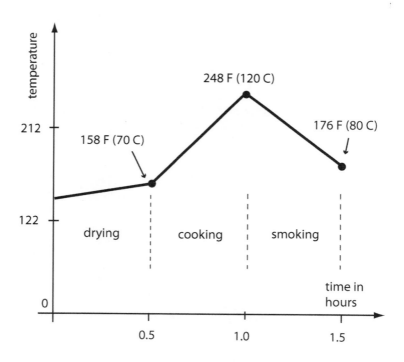

Fig. 5.9 Russian method of hot smoking fish.

Hot Smoking Fish at Home

Uniformity of smoking and drying is difficult to achieve in traditional wood fired smokers when products are placed on different levels. Fish on the bottom sticks will be dried while the fish higher up the smoker, surrounded by wet, steamy smoke that has already passed the fish below, will become wetter. Wet fish will attract more soot and unburned particles and its color is poorer. More heat is present in the back of the smoker than in the front. To compensate for these irregularities, the smoked products were rotated. The back of the fish or the skin of the fillet should face the back of the smoker. That allows for the better judgment of the fish color and protects the flesh from higher temperatures that are normally found in the back of the smoker.

When using a few levels of smokesticks insert the upper row first, then after 5-10 minutes the lower one, then the lowest one. If all three levels were placed in a smokehouse at the same time, the upper most row will get the least of the available heat during drying. On the other hand it will get the most moisture which it will gather from the smokesticks below.

Large heavy fish must be heat dried in a smokehouse before the smoke is applied. This hardens the fish and prevents them from falling down into the fire. A security screen should be positioned above the fire to catch any fish that might break free. Keep in mind that fat fish when hot smoked will drip some oil. If this oil drips into hot embers, the flames will shoot up and might even reach the fish above. Place an oil collecting aluminum foil pan between the fish and smoking wood. It may be placed on security screen.

A big advantage that a hobbyist has over a commercial producer is that he can experiment at will. He can introduce into the sawdust fresh herbs such as sage, rosemary, dill, crushed juniper berries, bay leaf or celery leaves. A typical process for hot smoking bigger fish (carp, eel, red fish):

- 1st hour- gradually increase the temperature to 158° F (70° C) to dry the fish.

- 2nd hour - smoke fish at 158-176° F (70-80° C).

- 3rd hour - cook/smoke fish at 212-230° F (100-110° C) for about 30 minutes. Switch off the heat add a few herbs to wood chips and smoke for another 15 minutes.

Photo 5.12 Smoking fish.

Smoking fish at higher temperatures drastically shortens the process. The fish can be smoked/baked in 30 minutes at 300-350° F (150-180° C), which can be considered barbecuing. Such a short time, however, will produce a little smoky flavor. The best course of action is to apply smoke for 60 minutes at 100-140° F (38-60° C) and then cook the fish at high temperatures. This can be easily accomplished even in a regular barbecue grill by filling with wood chips/sawdust a holed metal box, then placing it on hot charcoal briquettes. Once the chips ignite, they will keep on producing smoke. The simplest arrangement is to wrap up wooden chips with aluminium foil and make some holes in it with a nail. Ready to use cast iron or stainless steel cigar box sized containers are sold in the barbecue section of a large store. Do not wet your chips as this will create delay in producing smoke as moisture will have to evaporate first.

Photo 5.13 Smoking box.

Smokehouses for Hot Smoking

The most difficult part of hot smoking is maintaining temperature while burning wood chips. Using thermostat controlled electric heating elements simplifies the process but only for small units.

Photo 5.14 Burning whole logs is not easy and requires continuous attention.

A larger unit, like 20 cubic feet smoker below, needs powerful heating elements for hot smoking. Look at the modified warming oven that was converted into industrial quality smokehouse by Gary Zarebski of Winscosin.

Photo 5.15 The snow is on the ground, but this insulated smokehouse can maintain high temperatures in any conditions.

Photo 5.16 Hot plate for generating smoke and six powerful heating elements. A supply of 240 volt ectricity is needed.

Photo 5.17 Control panel is mounted on the side. The heat is, of course, automatically controlled by a thermostat.

Propane Fuel

If you live in cold climate and need a smokehouse that will work well, consider using propane gas. The design is very simple, a hole is drilled through the side of a smoking chamber and a gas delivery pipe is inserted. The inside of the pipe holds the burner, and the outside section is connected to a regulator and the tank.

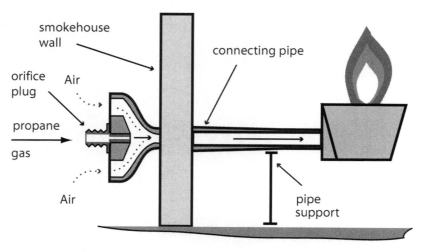

Fig. 5.10 A propane burner set up.

Photo 5.18 Threaded pipes of different length can be obtained in most hardware stores.

Photo courtesy Tejas Smokers.

Photo 5.19 Top view.

Photo 5.20 Pipe burners come in different length.

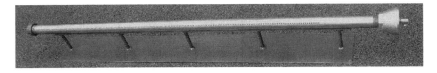

Photo 5.21 Pipe burner with support craddle.
Photo courtesy Tejas Smokers www.tejassmokers.com

Propane Heated Smokehouse

Photo 5.22 This 20 cubic feet smoker runs on propane. Note two thermometers.

Using propane gas offers the instant supply of huge amount of heat, fine control, inexpensive, portable - can be used in remote areas.

Photo 5.23 The outside connections.

Photo 5.24 Tejas Smokers 40,000 BTU burner.

Smoke Generator

Smoke can be generated by burning wood in a fire pit or by heating a metal pan filled with small wood chips or sawdust. Once they get hot enough they will produce smoke for 20-30 minutes.

An interesting approach is to connect a little smoke generator that works with an aquarium tank air pump. Such a smoke generator can be attached to any enclosure, including corrugated paper box.

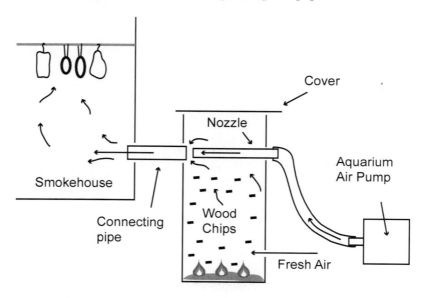

Fig. 5.11 Air pump smoke generator.

The pump delivers pressurized air into the smoking chamber. A vacuum forms in a little gap between the nozzle and the smokehouse connecting pipe. This vacuum pulls in smoke from burning wood chips and the rushing air delivers this smoke into the smokehouse. The smoke output is determined by turning the dial on the air pump that adjusts the speed of the air pump.

Photo 5.25 Smoke Daddy™ smoke generator.

Photo 5.26 The inside view of
the Smoke Daddy™ generator.

www.smokedaddyinc.com

Photo 5.27 The inside of the smokehouse, the burner and the smoke generator.

Be aware that propane gas burners provide a lot of heat. The 40,000 BTU burner pictured above is considered a small burner, but it is still the overkill for any smoker smaller than 20 cubic feet inside capacity. In warm weather it may be difficult to maintain temperatures of 140° F (60° C) or lower. For smaller smokers an electric heating element might be a better choice.

Thermometers

To be always on a safe side, use a common digital thermometer with a remote probe. Set the alarm to 145° F (63° C), insert the probe in a thickest part of the fish or fillet and start smoking. Once you hear the alarm, maintain this temperature for 30 minutes and you know the product is safely cooked. You may, however, continue smoking longer in order to obtain stronger smoky flavor. The control of the temperature is less important now, you may go higher, but try to stay at or above 145° F (63° C) internal meat temperature. At this temperature the food can be kept for a number of hours without the danger of bacterial growing again. At this temperature hot food is kept in restaurants.

Photo 5.29 The remote sensor.

Photo 5.28 Digital thermometer with remote sensor.

Factory Made Smokers

The big advantage of electric thermostatically controlled smokers is the ease with which the high temperatures can be maintained. However, small units have very little usable space inside, so you will not be able to hang a large fish.

Photo 5.30 The photo depicts a very well designed 20 lb. capacity insulated smoker made by the Sausage Maker, with the following features: 120 V, 800 W, heating element with an adjustable control, sawdust pan, smoke chimney with adjustable damper control, smoke diffuser, removable screens and smoke sticks for hanging meats and sausages. This unit is capable of maintaining internal temperatures of 160-170° F while the outdoor temperatures are as low as 5° F (-15° C).

Photo 5.31

This 100 lb. smoker comes with 220 V, 5000 W, heating element, thermostat control, electrical blower and built in smoke generator. Temp range 50-250°F.

Photo courtesy the Sausage Maker, Buffalo, N.Y.

Why Smoke Fish

You save money. Smoked fish is an expensive item as it requires time and extra processing steps. Compare the price of fresh and smoked salmon. It is still the same fish, but the price has doubled. You can smoke any fish you like. Manufacturers smoke and can fish that have proven to be profitable and accepted by majority of consumers. They will not take the risk of smoking red snapper, perch or scallops. In addition, some fish cannot be commercially traded, for example snook and red drum, but they can be caught for recreational use.

How Long to Smoke?

How long to smoke is an open question. Well, there isn't one universal time, use your own judgement and keep records. The size of the fish will be a deciding factor, but you can estimate smoking time by checking the color of the smoked fish as well. For example for a small fish like mullet 2-3 hours of hot smoking is plenty. It is safer to smoke for two hours and check the results. Over smoked fish will acquire a bitter smoked flavor that will not go away, so it is better to be on the safe side. A fish can be smoked and cooked within 20 minutes at 662° F (350° C), but its smoky flavor will be weak. Smoking needs time, about 2 hours will be sufficient for a typical size hot smoked fish. This implies that if you want to smoke one inch fillet for 2 hours, you have to choose smoking temperatures that will not overcook the fish.

When is the Fish Done?

The hot smoking process should finish at the high enough temperature to fully cook the meat and destroy the maximum number of bacteria. At 122° F (50° C) about 70-80% of fish proteins are cooked, but at 140° F (60° C) 95 % of proteins are fully cooked.

Cooking to 160° F (72° C) inside temperature produces the best tasting fish. Coincidentally, this is the recommended safe temperature for cooking red meats. The Food Safety and Inspection Service of the United States Department of Agriculture recommends cooking fish to 145° F (63° C) or higher for 30 minutes or longer.

Photo 5.32 Different size fish can be smoked at the same time, however, thicker fish will require longer processing time.

A reliable test is to insert a fork or knife into the thickest part of the fish and twist. The flesh should flake. In addition:

- the belly fin can be easily removed with fingers.
- the flesh of the belly must be white and not glassy.

It is difficult to hot smoke a large fish like carp or red fish in one piece. The solution is to split the fish lengthwise or cut across into steaks. Then, the fish can be smoked/cooked at 266° F (150° C) for about one hour. Basically, such method can be described as barbecuing fish with smoke.

Cooling

Smoked meats and sausages are usually showered with cold water to let them pass through the danger zone 60-140° F, (16-60° C) as fast as possible. Afterwards they can be refrigerated. The fish smoking process ends right inside the danger zone, so in order to preserve its useful life, the fish must be cooled quickly too.

Photo 5.33 Cooling smoked mullet.

Showering fish with water is not practical as much water will be trapped by the body of the fish. A better idea is to place fish in a drafty area or to use a ventilating fan to speed up cooling. Then the fish should be bagged and refrigerated or frozen. Hot smoked fish must be allowed to cool to at least room temperature, and preferably to about 32° F (0° C) in a cooler, before packing them. By room temperature we mean the temperature of around 68-77° F (20-25° C). Fish that is vacuum packed or packed into ziplock bags warm will turn flabby and sour, and may turn moldy.

Packing and Storing

Fish can be eaten immediately after smoking though many people say that it tastes better when cold. Fish should be wrapped up in wax paper or foil and placed in a refrigerator where it can remain for up to 10 days. To hold it longer we have to freeze it.

Photo 5.34 Packing smoked mullet into sealable plastic bags.

Hot smoked products made from white fish generally keep better than those made from fatty fish, although shelf life will vary considerably, depending on the amounts of salt and smoke present, the degree of drying, and the storage temperature. At a chill temperature of about 38 F (3° C) fatty products will keep in good condition for about 6 days and white fish products for about 8 days; at 50° F (10° C) the shelf life is reduced to 2-3 days for fatty fish and 4-5 days for white fish.

Hot smoked products can be frozen and kept in cold store at -22° F (-30° C) for at least 6 months, and for longer when vacuum packed. Products with a high fat content are inclined to have a soft texture after freezing and thawing. Salted fish should be stored in a cool, dark place, especially if it is fat. The rate of spoilage in salt fish doubles with each 15° F; salt fish kept at 95° F (35° C) will spoil twice as fast as the fish kept at 80° F (27° C). Keep salt fish at low temperatures where it can remain up to 2 years. The fish can be stored in strong brine at low temperatures, but it must be submerged.

Type of Smoke

We can control to a certain degree the quality of the smoke. The smoke can be wet or dry. Wet smoke is produced when the rate of combustion is low. This happens when a small amount of air is allowed to enter smoke generation unit. Using small chips, especially sawdust will result in a low combustion and heavy smoke. Adding wet sawdust will produce even more wet smoke. Wet smoke attracts more resinous and unburnt particles. As a result when smoking time is long, the product may acquire a bitter taste. Dry smoke is produced by a more complete combustion. The smoke is lighter and the smoked product develops a good flavor and color. Burning larger chips, chunks or even log wood will provide more access for the air to enter the burning pile and will result in hotter and cleaner smoke.

Humidity

Commercial smokehouses are equipped with temperature and humidity controls. In many smokehouses, the efficiency of the operation is still dependent on atmospheric conditions. The air can be moist or dry. When the air is moist the moisture can be removed from the air before it enters the smoking chamber. This could be accomplished by installing a cooling system ahead the incoming air. If the air is passed over crushed ice it will be cooled as well. The cold air cannot hold moisture anymore and we are left with cold dry air. If this air is preheated now, the very dry but hot smoke will enter the smoking chamber. When the air is too dry, for example smoking during the day in desert area, a pan filled with water may be inserted into smoking chamber. Presoaking wood chips will bring some moisture, but only for a while. Air speed should not be too great otherwise excessive drying of the product results. In home smokehouses the natural draft (air velocity) can be controlled with exit dampers. Humidity is higher at night than during the day. If the weather is warm and humid, the heat transfer is more rapid and the meat will cook faster.

Color of Smoked Fish

The color of smoked fish depends on the color of the skin, the length of smoking process and the type of the wood used for smoke generation. Mullet, herring, blue fish, or mackerel, all have different color of the skin and flesh, so they will have a distinctive color after smoking.

Dark colored fish will be dark after smoking and silver colored fish will develop golden or light brown color. The type of wood will contribute to the final color, although up to a certain point.

Color	Wood
yellow-lemon	acacia
gold-yellow	maple, linden, beech
yellow-brown	oak, alder, walnut
reddish	hickory

The color, however, will become darker as the smoking goes on, for example, the light colored fish may be develop yellow color that will change to light brown and brown color as the process continues.

Wood for Smoking

Any *hardwood* is fine, but evergreen trees like fir, spruce, pine, or others cause problems. They contain too much resin and the finished product has a turpentine flavor to it. It also develops a black color due to the extra soot from the smoke, which in turn makes the smoker dirtier too. And of course you cannot use any wood that was previously pressure treated, painted, or commercially manufactured. The type of wood used is responsible for the final color of the smoked product and it can also influence its taste but only to a small degree. The type of hardwood used for smoking is not as important as people like to imagine. All fruit and citrus trees have a light to medium sweet flavor and are excellent for poultry and ham. Many say that cherry wood is the best.

It is a fact that alder was popular for smoking salmon in Pacific Northwest and it is a fact that it is popular in Poland by both, the hobbyist and commercial producers. However, alder wood owes its popularity not to any secret components in its composition, but to a simple fact that is plentiful in those areas. It grows well there and it produces satisfactory smoke.

The popularity of a particular wood is directly related to the fact whether it grows in a particular area. It will be most illogical to order wood over Internet when a local hardwood is free for the picking. Beech is common in Germany in Poland, and is used by commercial plants, very often mixed half and half with alder. Alder, oak and poplar are popular in Russia.

Oak was popular for cold smoking fish in England, and still is the best wood all around. Many wood chip manufacturers stay away from oak as it makes their cutting saws dull in no time at all. However, if you are willing to use an ax and cut some oak chips, it is a great wood for smoking. Oak will paint the product brown.

Hickory is good, but unknown outside the USA. Hickory leaves a reddish tint.

Fruit and nut trees are good for smoking, however, not so abundant as grown in the wild alder or oak. This makes them expensive.

Combining different woods will create customized tints of color, for example oak and hickory will produce a pretty reddish-brown color. Walnut, which has a heavy smoke flavor, can be mixed with apple wood to create a milder version. Alder imparts yellow color so it is especially good for fish. Keep in mind that the deepness of color is related to the length of smoking.

Avoid using soft woods like pine, cedar, spruce and most ever green needle trees. Those trees will produce dark color. Resins from these trees will leave unpleasant flavor on the fish. Be smart, use hardwood which is available for free. The quality of smoked fish depends more on curing or drying than on a type of wood used for smoking.

Note: always store sawdust very dry. Sawdust is very dense and easily develops moisture pockets which can hold large numbers of mold spores. These molds can adhere to the surface of the fish during smoking and can multiply during storage. The shelf life of the product will be greatly decreased.

SMOKING SHELLFISH

Shellfish such as mussels, clams, oysters and shrimp are very delicate and require short brining and smoking times. Overcooking makes them rubbery. Detailed instructions are included in the recipe section.

Photo 5.35 Shrimp and scallops. **Photo 5.36** Serving shellfish.

Canning Fish *(Adapted from "Home Canning Meat, Poultry, Fish and Vegetables")*

Neither the FDA nor the USDA/FSIS have jurisdiction over foods that are canned at home. This creates big safety problems for low acid-products such as meat, poultry, *fish* and vegetables that are produced at home. Too often, home canners who have produced jams in the past incorrectly assume that all foods can be processed with the same procedure. This may in part be attributed to the insufficient information on the subject of canning low-acid foods that has been written for a home canner, but ultimately, the responsibility rests with the person who makes the product. He cannot blame his ignorance on the canning techniques of his mother or grandmother, as they did not have access to the information that is in abundance today. *It is his duty to learn the basic rules of canning before he attempts to make a product.*

Almost all cases of food poisoning can be traced to canned food produced at home. It is very rare that a commercial plant will employ incorrect procedures or use a faulty recipe. The commercial packers work under such tight regulations and inspection programs, that any violation of the process is usually the product of a human error.

The thermal resistance of microorganisms decreases as the pH of their medium is lowered. Most bacteria, particularly *Cl. botulinum*, will not grow below pH 4.6. Therefore acidic foods having pH below 4.6 do not require as severe heat treatment as those with pH above 4.6 (low acid) to achieve microbiological safety.

The pH value of 4.6 is the division between high acid foods and low acid foods. Low-acid foods have pH values higher than 4.6. They include red meats, *seafood*, poultry, milk, and all fresh vegetables except for most tomatoes.

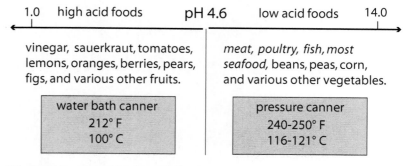

Fig 5.12 Low and high acid foods.

Meats, poultry, *fish* and vegetables are classified as low-acid foods (pH > 4.6) and must be processed until a condition of *"commercial sterility"* is achieved. Commercial sterility is defined as the condition obtained by the application of heat alone or in combination with other treatments to render the product free of microorganisms capable of growing in the product at normal *non-refrigerated* conditions. The product is safe to eat because the pathogenic microorganisms are either destroyed or inactivated to the extent that they pose no health risk. The product will remain shelf stable as long as the container is perfectly sealed, which is what prevents the entry of any microorganisms from the outside. Since spoilage bacteria are easily killed during heat treatment, the product has an almost unlimited shelf life as long as it is stored at proper conditions.

Safety of Canned Products - It Is All About *Clostridium Botulinum*

Where most bacteria can be killed at 160° F, 72° C, *Cl. botulinum* is protected inside of the spore and will survive the temperature of boiling water (212° F, 100° C) for 5 hours. Processing meat for so long will result in a poor texture, flavor and color. For this reason low acid foods must be processed in a pressure canner at 240° F, 116° C as this temperature will kill botulinum spores in about 2 minutes. If spores are not completely killed in canned foods, vegetative microorganisms will grow from the spores as soon as conditions are favorable again.

Time and Temperature Needed to Deactivate *Cl. botulinum* Spores		
214° F, 101° C	232° F, 111° C	250° F, 121° C
250 min	25 min	2.5 min

Now, we finally know that the biggest enemy of canned foods is *Clostridium botulinum*, a dangerous heat resistant microorganism which *does not need oxygen to grow.* If a canned product does not receive proper heat treatment, there is an increased risk that *Cl.botulinum* could survive and *produce toxin* within a container. The thermal resistance of microorganisms decreases as the pH of their medium is lowered. As explained earlier, most bacteria, particularly *Cl. botulinum*, will not grow below pH 4.6. Therefore acidic foods having pH below 4.6 do not require as severe heat treatment as those with pH above 4.6 (low acid) to achieve microbiological safety.

Control of *Cl.botulinum*

There are two ways of controlling *Cl.botulinum*:

- Killing spores.
- Preventing spores from germinating and growing.

Spores of *Cl.botulinum* are present in both acidic and low-acid foods. In low acid-foods such as meats and vegetables, *Cl.botulinum* spores can only be killed at 240° F, 116° C or higher. The high acidity (pH < 4.6), however, prevents botulinum bacteria from leaving the spores. This prevents them from germinating and growing, and of course no toxin is produced. For this reason *high-acid foods* such as fruits or juices can be processed at 212° F, 100° C as this temperature will kill all bacteria in vegetative form and bacterial spores are prevented from germinating by high acidity.

The growth of *Cl.botulinum* is inhibited at 10% salt concentration which is equivalent to a water activity of around 0.93. Obviously, such high salt percentages will not be tolerated by a consumer.

Low-acid foods must be processed in a pressure canner to be free of botulism risks.

There is a small dilemma when the subject of low-acid recipes comes around as there are very few recipes available for a home canner. Please use recipes that come from *reputable source,* like the USDA's canning guides and bulletins. The USDA *"Complete Guide to Home Canning," Agriculture Information Bulletin No. 539, USDA, revised 2009,* has been the oldest and most reliable publication on the subject of canning. It was issued first time in 1909 as the *Farmer's Bulletin 359,* by the Bureau of Chemistry.

Photo 5.37 Presto pressure canner. Fish packed in glaas jars or metal cans must be processed in a pressure canner.

Photo 5.38 Ives-Way can sealer.

Summary of Critical Issues

- Smoke is inhibited by the skin and the scales.

- Smoke is inhibited by the fat, lean fish smokes faster.

- The more air available to wood for smoking, the higher the temperature. Burning sawdust results in the lowest temperature, and the densest, but the dirtiest smoke. A lot of soot is produced.

- Hardwoods produce the cleanest smoke.

- Evergreen coniferous and needle type trees are rich in resin and produce low quality, turpentine flavor smoke.

- Dry wood should be used for cold smoking.

- Soaked wood chips may be used for hot smoking.

- Wet wood produces smoke that is rich in vapor, soot, and many unburnt particles. The smoke is dark, heavy, consisting of large particles.

- Meats with wet surface acquire smoke faster, unfortunately the heavier particles and soot are easily attracted. The resulting color is dark and the flavor inferior.

- The fish that was dried before smoking will develop the most attractive color.

- The smoked fish develops the best color in about 2 hours, however, after the process is stopped, the development of color will still continue and will be the strongest after about 10 hours.

- A darker color develops when the smoking time is increased and the thicker smoke is applied. Increasing the smoking time and applying the thinner smoke will produce the same results as decreasing the smoking time and applying the denser smoke.

- The best quality fish is produced when hot smoke does not exceed 180° F (82° C).

Chapter 6

Recipes

Majority of people buy a fish to cook a dinner. The fish is steamed, fried, baked or barbecued and served on a plate with fries, rice and vegetables. They may throw a few wood chips on hot charcoals, but this is hardly smoking fish. You need 1-2 hours to develop smoky flavor and obviously you cannot torture the fish for two hours on the grill. Fresh fish or frozen fillets can be purchased in a supermarket and smoked in small commercially produced smokers, which will do a reasonably good job of smoking a fish or two. Then they can be eaten, hot, cold or prepared as a pate. It is fast, convenient, but costly.

People who catch their own fish may end up with many fish at one trip. It is not unusual to catch 100 mullets with one throw of a castnet in Florida. We must not forget those living in remote areas of Alaska who need game meat and a lot of fish fish to survive in winter. If you process 50 or more fish in one day, it will be time consuming to dry salt each fish so use brine. By the time the fish are gutted, the 80° brine is prepared and all is needed is to dump the fish into the brine. Needless to say, a large brine container and about 20 cubic feet smokehouse is needed for handling such a load.

It will be boring to eat the same style smoked fish on a regular basis, hence the smoked fish becomes the basic ingredient that will end up in spreads, pates, mousses or be served with different sauces. As a result, the same type of fish looks and tastes different.

The brining and smoking parameters can be
varied to suit particular tastes.

A person smoking a few fish at the time can improvise a lot with selection of spices and other ingredients. Having a fish or two that do not meet our expectations is not as bad as ruining taste of many fish. For a large batch production the best advice is to use salt only. You cannot ruin fish by salting and smoking alone as long as you apply correct amount of salt and smoke fish at the right temperature.

Before serving the fish can be seasoned anyway you like, topped with a sauce of your choice or served cold or hot on lettuce or a toast. Keep it simple: fresh fish, salt and smoke, and you will get the top quality product. Some fish like *cold smoked* salmon do not need any help at all. They are simply perfect and they need only a roll with butter or cream cheese. As salmon goes well with dill, a dill sauce is a good compliment to a baked or hot smoked salmon. There are some who complain that all fish taste the same. Some fish, like mullet, salmon or mackerel have a distinctive flavor, but others display less character and their flavor may be enriched by:

- Sauce. Serving fish with a sauce that complements its flavor. This is the easiest way to augment the flavor of the fish.

- Making spread or mousse. This can be a simple spread or savory fish mousse, all depends how fancy we want to be. Now, we can create the smoked fish art that will impress all.

In recipes you can substitute one type of the fish for the other, for example flounder, sole or halibut are very similar. Cod, haddock, pollock and whiting are also similar lean fish. Then you have oily fish like bluefish, mackerel or eel. Trout and salmon have similar characteristics. When in doubt consult the table in Chapter 1 which lists fat content of different fish.

Sauces for Smoked Fish

A sauce provides an individual character to a steamed fish. Adding sauce to poached, fried or baked fish drastically changes its appearance and flavor and makes the dish more appealing. Place a piece of fried fish on a plate and it will remain just a piece of ordinary fried fish. Pour some sauce over it, add a sliced lemon, sprig of parsley and it becomes a dish. Although the idea of making sauce may seem intimidating to some, on the contrary, making sauces is fast and easy. There are no fixed rules, but the white fish agree best with delicate cream sauces and herb butters, whereas oily fish like mackerel or salmon can take stronger flavors. There are some flavors such as lemon juice or dill that can be used with white wine sauces, or creamy butters to serve with whole fish, fillets and steaks whether just cooked or smoked.

Sauce Making

Many sauces use one basic foundation sauce known as "drawn butter." It also goes by the name of "roux", which is basically thickening used for making soups, gravies and sauces.

- In making a sauce which contains egg yolks for thickening, the sauce must not boil after they are added or it will curdle. Take care to remember that eggs will not thicken in a mixture unless the boiling point is nearly reached. The sauce must be carefully watched and at the first sign of boiling draw it aside where it cannot boil, then add the egg yolks and keep it where the temperature will be just under the boiling point. Remember that after the egg yolks are added, the sauce must never be left where it may boil again.

- In adding butter to a sauce, drop it in a small piece at a time, stirring each time until blended before adding another piece. If too much butter is added to a sauce all at once it might cause it to separate from the sauce, so for that reason it should be added gradually.

- Do not prepare sauces until you are ready to use them, but when they must be kept hot, place the saucepan in boiling water, where the sauce may be kept under the boiling point.

- Commercially made fish sauce may be used as a base in creating many of your own sauces.

- Tabasco pepper sauce or cayenne pepper can be added to any sauce to spice it up.

Notes: to soften butter take it out of refrigerator and leave for one hour at room temperature.

Fish Spreads

Making smoked fish spreads offers many advantages:

- You get more product when smoked fish is mixed with other materials.

- Fish spreads taste great.

- Smoked fish spreads are very expensive so you end up with a product that you might be hesitant to buy.

It does not matter much whether you call them spreads, pastes or pates. Pates are usually made with livers so we have decided to call the product the spread. Smoked fish makes wonderful spreads. Oily fish contains more fat and so it is easier to spread, however, lean fish is also spreadable as butter, cream, cream cheese or yogurt will make a great paste.

Common ingredients: butter, cream cheese, sour cream, meat stock (consomme), plain yogurt, mayonnaise and avocado pulp. They can be added on their own or mixed together. It makes little difference whether you use plain yogurt or sour cream.

Flavorings: pepper, onion, garlic, cayenne, chives, parsley, dill, curry, lemon, mushrooms.

Smoked fish trimmings should account for at least 50% of the total ingredients, otherwise the flavor of smoked fish may be hard to sense. To a certain degree you can influence the color of a spread. For example in curry spread the color is yellowish due to the "turmeric" spice which is always present in curry mixtures. If you add more turmeric the color will be a stronger yellow. Paprika may be added as well and the color will be dark orange. Smoked paprika (pimento) has a deep red color so the color will be stronger. Another interesting spice is "annatto" which has a very dark red color. One teaspoon added to 8 oz mullet spread will introduce a pink tint in the spread. Avocado is of course green so the spread will appear greenish.

Food processors are of great help when making spreads. If you make a lot of spread, it is helpful to pre-grind fish trimmings with a manual grinder. Then you can finish the process using a food processor or mix everything together in a bowl.

Fish Mousse

Mousse is a light creamy dish made from fish and set with gelatin. Most of us a familiar with a chocolate mousse, a popular desert, but mousse can be made with vegetables, meat or fish. Mousse becomes light and fluffy by beating cream and eggs what generates air pockets inside. The gelatin helps ingredients stick together, however, eggs alone will bind the ingredients as well. Savory mousses are usually cooked in water bath and they can be served hot or cold. A mousse is often served with a sauce that is designed to bring out the flavor of the fish.

Fish Salads

Making a salad does not need much introduction. This is where lean smoked fish may be as good as oily ones, if not better. Fat smoked fish carries stronger flavor as the fat is the component that carries meat flavor. You can use stronger spices with fat smoked fish such as curry, mustard, ginger, hot peppers or horseradish. With lean fish you may strive for a more delicate balance. Potatoes, noodles, rice, eggs, mayonnaise, onions, peppers, celery, parsley, are often used in salads.

We have limited our recipes to cold servings only, a few hot sandwiches being the exception. Dishes that require baking in the oven, for example a fish casserole are not included as we feel it is a waste of smoked fish to be used in a such a way. Regular or smoked fish can be used in salads.

Fancy Arrangements

Smoked fish can presented and arranged in beautiful and unique ways. All smoked meats such as hams, sausages, liver pates, head cheeses and meat jellies are usually served cold for a simple reason; they taste better when cold. Smoked fish conforms to the same rule and in majority cases are served cold. Baked in oven, barbecued or grilled fish are fish dishes which are served hot. They may have a faint smoky flavor if wood chips were added to hot charcoal, but they do not develop the same flavor as the properly smoked fish. Serving fish cold offers a big advantage: the fish can be prepared beforehand. Very fancy arrangements can be prepared in advance of the meal and the dishes can be beautifully garnished.

Bits of smoked fish can be placed on small toasts and topped with a sauce. Spreads and dips can be placed in cocktail and wine glasses and topped with fish roe. Pulp can be removed from tomatoes, cucumbers, baked potatoes, apples, and they can be filled with fish spreads. Citrus fruit like lemons, grapefruit or oranges can be halved, emptied, filled with fish spreads and garnished with dill or parsley. How far you want to go is limited only by your imagination and how much you want to impress your guests.

Photo 6.1 Scallops with orange sauce.

Photo 6.2 Fish spreads filled with avocado and lemon.

Recipe Index

33	Large Roe, cooked	226
34	Large Roe, with Bacon	226
35	Mullet Roe	228
36	Mullet Milt	229
37	Salad of Fish Roe	227
38	Small Pieces of Roe	227
39	Creamed Roe on Toast	227
40	Scalloped Roe and Oysters	227
41	Flounder or Sole Roe, Creamed with Green Peas	229
42	Creamed Roe, with Shrimps	229
43	Creamed Milt on Toast	229
Spreads, Mousses and Dips		
44	Bluefish Spread	140
45	Catfish Sandwiches	144
46	Flounder Avocado Cocktail	152
47	Mackerel Deviled Spread	167
48	Mackerel Horseradish Spread	167
49	Mackerel Pate	167
50	Mullet Avocado	174
51	Mullet Cream Cheese	174
52	Mullet Curry Spread	174
53	Mullet Dip	175
54	Mullet Guacamole	175
55	Mullet Horseradish	176
56	Mullet Mousse	176
57	Mullet Soft Spread	176
58	Salmon Avocado	190
59	Salmon Bechamel	186
60	Salmon Cream Cheese	187
61	Salmon Dip	187
62	Salmon Mousse with Dill Sauce	189
63	Salmon Pate	190
64	Tilapia Mousse	195
65	Trout Cucumber Spread	199
66	Tuna Dip	203
67	Tuna Mousse	205
68	Tuna Pineapple Dip	206

	Salads and Sandwiches	
69	Bluefish with Sour Cream and Beets	140
70	Cod Deviled Salad	147
71	Eel with Sour Cream	150
72	Halibut Jellied Salad	157
73	Halibut Jellied Pineapple Salad	157
74	Salmon a la King	185
75	Salmon Canapes	186
76	Salmon Club Sandwich	187
77	Salmon Salad	188
78	Salmon Stuffed Tomatoes Salad	188
79	Tuna a la King	201
80	Tuna a la Stroganoff	201
81	Tuna Canapes with Mushrooms	202
82	Tuna Canapes Tangy	202
83	Tuna Cheese Sandwich	203
84	Tuna Jambalaya	204
85	Tuna Molded Salad	204
86	Tuna Salad	206
87	Tuna Slaw	207
88	Tuna Souffle Salad	207
89	Tuna Tossed Salad	208
90	Tuna with Noodles	208
91	Tuna with rRce	209
92	Tuna Waldorf Salad	209
93	Whiting Salad	210
	Sauces for Smoked Fish	
94	Aioli	231
95	Anchovy	231
96	Bechamel	232
97	Caper	230
98	Celery Cream	234
99	Citrus	234
100	Cocktail Sauce	234
101	Cucumber	235
102	Curry	235
103	Drawn Butter (Roux)	230

104	Egg	236
105	Hollandaise	236
106	Horseradish	236
107	Mayonnaise	237
108	Mushroom	237
109	Mustard	238
110	Orange	238
111	Oyster	239
112	Parsley Sauce	230
113	Parsley Cream Sauce	239
114	Red Devil	240
115	Supreme	240
116	Tartar Sauce	240
117	Thick White Sauce	241
118	Tomato Cream	241
119	Tomato Curry	242
120	Velote Sauce	242
Cold Butter Sauces		
121	Anchovy Butter	243
122	Curry Butter	243
123	Dill Butter	243
124	Garlic Butter	244
125	Ginger Butter	244
126	Horseradish Butter	244
127	Lemon Butter	244
128	Parsley Butter	244
129	Wasabi Butter	244

Bluefish *(Pomatomus saltatrix)*

Name	Protein %	Fat %	Water %
Bluefish	20.04	4.24	70.86

Photo 6.3 Due to its high fat content, bluefish is delicious when smoked.

Bluefish are widely distributed around the world in tropical and sub-tropical waters. Along the U.S. east coast, bluefish make seasonal migrations north in the spring and south in the winter. Some bluefish remain in the Gulf of Mexico throughout the year. Bluefish are one of the most popular recreational species along the Atlantic coast.

Smoking Bluefish

Fillet the fish. Leave the skin on as the flesh is delicate.
Brine 1/2" fillets for 5 minutes in 80° brine. Wash and drain.
Dry fillets for 30 minutes in a smokehouse preheated to 100° F (38° C).
Smoke for 60 minutes at 185° F (85° C).
Switch off the heat and smoke for 15 minutes more.

Photo 6.4 Adult bluefish are typically between 8" - 24" (20 - 60 cm) long. Bluefish has enough flesh to be filleted.

Bluefish with Sour Cream and Beets

8 oz smoked bluefish fillets
3 Tbsp chopped beets
3 Tbsp sour cream
1 Tbsp chopped onion
1 tsp dried dill
1 Tbsp vinegar
1 tsp prepared mustard
2 Tbsp olive oil
1 tsp sugar
Salt and pepper to taste

Dressing. Mix together mustard, vinegar, sour cream, dill, chopped onions and olive oil. Add salt, pepper and sugar. Add chopped beets. Fry a slice of bread in olive oil on both sides.
Serve fillets with browned slices of bread and the dressing.

Bluefish Spread

Smoked bluefish (1 lb)
3 oz butter
6 Tbsp plain yogurt
3 Tbsp creamed horseradish
1 Tbsp lemon juice

Flake bluefish and grind it.
Mix with all ingredients until a paste is obtained.

Carp (*Cyprinus carpio*)

Name	Protein %	Fat %	Water %
Carp	17.83	5.60	76.31

The common carp is native to Asia, and has been introduced to every part of the world. Carp is eaten in many parts of the world both when caught from the wild and raised in aquaculture. In countries such as Poland, Germany, Czech Republic, Slovakia and Hungary, carp is a traditional part of a Christmas Eve dinner. Carp is omnivorous; it can eat variety of foods, grass included. It can survive in water with little oxygen and that is why it has been farmed in ponds for over 2,000 years. Due to the facts that carp is great survivor and that a single carp can lay over a million eggs in a year, the fish is known to take over a particular body of water. For these reasons carp is often considered an invasive species.

The annual production of common carp in China alone exceeds the weight of all other fish, such as trout and salmon, produced by aquaculture worldwide. Carp can become quite large fish, the world record is 101 pounds (46 kg).

Photo 6.5 Common carp have an even, regular scale pattern.

Creator: Raver, Duane, U.S. Fish and Wildlife Service

Photo 6.6 Mirror carp are commonly found in the United Kingdom and Europe. The body is covered by few scales that resemble little mirrors.

Creator: Raver, Duane, U.S. Fish and Wildlife Service

Photo 6.7 Big Muddy National Wildlife Refuge, Missouri, employees hold an Asian carp.

U.S. Fish and Wildlife Service

Hot Smoked Carp

Remove scales, cut off the head and gut the fish. Wash thoroughly. Cut into chunks between 1/2 and 1 pound.
Brine for 8 hours in 80° brine. Rinse and drain.
Apply a thin smoke at 100° F (38° C) for 60 minutes.
Increase the temperature to 185° F (85° C) and smoke with medium smoke for 120 minutes.

Paprika Carp

Four pound of carp, 4 Tbsp butter, 2 chopped onions, 3 Tbsp Hungarian paprika, 1 clove garlic, 1 chopped green pepper, 1 peeled and chopped tomato, 1/3 cup white wine, 1/2 tsp pepper, 1 Tbsp lemon juice.

Sauté onion in butter until light brown, add garlic, paprika, wine, mix and simmer for 1-2 minutes. Add green pepper and tomato, cover and simmer for 15 minutes. Place smoked carp on top and simmer for additional 5 minutes. Sprinkle with lemon juice and serve.

Catfish

Name	Protein %	Fat %	Water %
Catfish, wild	16.38	2.82	80.36
Catfish, farmed	15.23	5.94	79.06

Catfish live inland or in coastal waters all over the world. They have no scales but their skin is tough and hard to penetrate. Named for their prominent barbels, which resemble a cat's whiskers, catfish range in size and weight. The average size of the species is about 3.9–5.2 ft (1.2–1.6 m). In North America large catfish can weigh well over 100 pounds, however, the record belong to Thailand giant Mekong catfish that weighed 650 lb (293 kg).

Photo 6.8 Channel-catfish.

U.S. Fish and Wildlife Service

Hot Smoked Catfish

Skin the fish and gut it. Cut the fish into 1 pound chunks.
Brine for 8 hours in 80° brine. Rinse and drain.
Air dry for 1 hour.
Apply a thin smoke at 100° F (38° C) for 2 hours.
Increase the temperature to 176° F (80° C) and smoke for 2 more hours.

Farm Raised Catfish Fillets

Brine fillets for 5 minutes in 80° brine. Wash and drain.
Dry fillets for 30 minutes in a smokehouse preheated to 100° F (38° C).
Smoke for 60 minutes at 185° F (85° C).
Switch off the heat and smoke for 15 minutes more.

Catfish Sandwiches

2 cups flaked smoked catfish
1/4 cup sliced stuffed olives
1/2 cup chopped celery
1 teaspoon grated onion
1/2 cup mayonnaise
1 teaspoon Worcestershire sauce
1/2 teaspoon salt
Dash pepper
1/2 teaspoon prepared mustard
Bread toast

Combine all ingredients except bread. Chill.
Spread bread with fish mixture; cover with another bread toast.

Photo 6.9 Mike Mangold with blue catfish at Dyke Marsh, Virginia.
U.S. Fish and Wildlife Service

Cod *(Gadus morhua)*

Name	Protein %	Fat %	Water %
Cod, Atlantic	17.81	0.67	81.22
Cod, Pacific	15.27	0.41	83.95

The cod we are referring to in our book is the Atlantic cod *(Gadus morhua),* the fish popular in Europe and North America. There are other cod species the Pacific cod, *(Gadus macrocephalus)* or the poor cod *(Gadus minutus)* which is a much smaller relative of the Atlantic cod. The cod is typically a bottom-living fish that live in cold water 30-50° F (-1 - 10° C). The cod will eat almost any marine animal including other cod, but it feeds mainly on the smaller fatty fishes such as herring, sand eels, and on shrimp and squid.

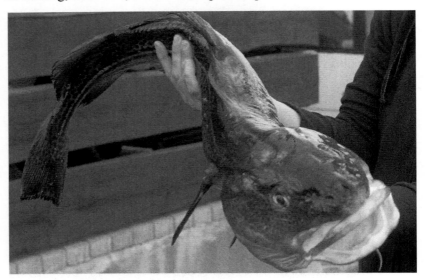

Photo 6.10 Baltic Sea cod. The cod is the leanest of all fish.

The two most important species of cod are the Atlantic cod (Gadus morhua), which lives in the colder waters and deeper sea regions throughout the North Atlantic, and the Pacific cod (Gadus macrocephalus), found in both eastern and western regions of the northern Pacific. Cod is popular as a food with a mild flavour and a dense, flaky white flesh. Cod livers are processed to make cod liver oil, an important source of vitamin A, vitamin D, vitamin E and omega-3 fatty acids. Haddock and whiting belong in the same family, the Gadidae, as cod. The Atlantic cod weighs 5–12 kilograms (11–26 lb), but specimens weighing up to 100 kilograms (220 lb) have been recorded. Pacific cod are smaller than their Atlantic cod and are darker in color.

Cod Fillets *(Cold Smoked)*

Cod fillets are normally skinned as the flesh is firm. The fillets are brined in 80° brine for from 4-10 minutes depending upon size. The brined fillets are placed on screens and allowed to drip for at least two hours before smoking. The fillets are smoked at 80° F (27° C) from two to five hours depending on on the size.

Smoked Cod Fillets.

Brine the 1/2" fillets for 5 minutes in 80° brine. Wash and drain. Place on oiled screens.
Dry fillets for 30 minutes in a smokehouse preheated to 100° F (38° C).
Smoke for 60 minutes at 185° F (85° C). Switch off the heat and smoke for 15 minutes more.

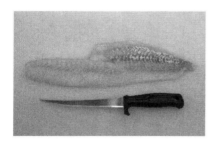

Photo 6.11 Cod fillet.

Cod Deviled Salad

2 cups flaked smoked cod	1/4 cup bell pepper
2 cups diced cooked potatoes	1/4 cup raw carrot
1/2 cup diced celery	1/4 cup mayonnaise
1/4 cup diced onions	1 teaspoon prepared mustard
	1 teaspoon tabasco sauce

Mix smoked fish with all vegetables.
Blend mayonnaise, mustard and tabasco sauce together.
Combine everything together.

Eel *(Anguilla anguilla)*

Name	Protein %	Fat %	Water %
Eel	18.44	11.66	68.26

The eel has an elongated snake-like body, tapering almost to a point at the tail. Although the eel is very slimy and appears to be scaleless, scales are deeply embedded in some parts of the skin. There is a pair of pectoral fins just behind the small head, and there is a small gill opening just in front of each fin. The back fin and the anal fin are very long and merge with the tail fin to form a continuous soft-rayed fin fringe. Eels generally range from 15" (40 cm) to 30" (80 cm) and 8 oz (250 g) to 2.2 lb (1 kg) in weight.

Photo 6.12 Smoked eels.

Killing and Cleaning

The simplest method of killing eels is to put them in a deep container and rouse them with salt; leave them for up to 2 hours to kill them and to remove much of the slime. They should not be completely buried in salt; a good sprinkling is sufficient. They may lose up to 5 percent in weight during this stage. Another method of rapidly removing slime is to immerse the eels in 1 percent ammonia solution, made by adding one part of ammonia liquor to 100 parts of water. Newly killed eels should be washed thoroughly in clean water; up to half an hour in cold water, followed by very careful scraping. It is recommended to *scrub the skin* to give a good appearance to the finished product.

Smoked Eel

Eel is a fatty fish and is an absolute delicacy when smoked. The fish is very slimy and the best way to remove this sticky substance is by wiping it off with sand, sawdust, newspapers or paper towels. Rinse with water. Slit the belly 1 inch (25 mm) or so beyond the vent in order to remove the kidney; scrub the gut cavity and wash it out carefully to remove all traces of blood from the backbone and throat, and then rinse the eels again. Heads are not removed.

Immerse eels in 80° brine (275 g salt per one liter of water) for 15 minutes. Excessive salting results in white spots appearing on the skin of the fish during smoking.

Thread the brined eels on 1/4" (6 mm) diameter rods or speats by pushing the pointed end of the rod through the throat from front to back. Place small lengths of stick between the belly flaps to keep them apart; this allows smoke to penetrate the belly cavity.

Preheat the smokehouse and smoke the eels:

1 hour at 90° F (35°C).
1 hour at 122° F (50°C).
1 hour at 185° (85)°C.

Cook the fish until the belly opens wide and there are no red areas. To check whether the fish is cooked, press on its sides and the meat should separate from the backbone. A few little perpendicular wrinkles should appear behind the head.

The eels should lose about 15-20 per cent by weight during the smoking operation. Cool and cut into smaller sections.

Photo 6.13 Smoked eel.

Photo 6.14 Smoked eel with the skin removed.

Eel with Sour Cream

8 oz smoked eel fillets
3 Tbsp chopped beets
3 Tbsp sour cream
1 Tbsp vinegar
1 tsp prepared mustard
2 hard boiled eggs
2 Tbsp olive oil
1 tsp sugar
Salt and pepper to taste

Rub egg yolks through a sieve. Chop egg whites finely.

Dressing

Mix together egg yolks, mustard, vinegar, sour cream and olive oil.
Add salt, pepper and sugar. Add chopped beets.
Place each fillet on a plate and surround with dressing. Sprinkle with chopped egg white.
Fry a slice of bread in olive oil on both sides.
Serve fillets with browned slices of bread.

Flounder *(Paralichthys albiguttata)*

Name	Protein %	Fat %	Water %
Flounder	12.41	1.93	84.63

Photo 6.15 & 6.16 Adam Marianski holding a large Floridian gulf flounder.

Flounder is a bottom feeding flat fish found at the bottom of coastal lagoons and estuaries of the Northern Atlantic and Pacific Oceans. The European flounder is found in the colder waters around Northern Europe. Sole is a type of flounder common in European waters. The Gulf flounder *(Paralichthys albiguttata)* is common on the west coast of Florida.

Cold-Smoked Flounder

Small flounder, about 1/2 pound. Gut the fish, brine for 2 hours in 90° brine. Insert the fish on rods, drain and air dry for 2 hours. Smoke with cold smoke for 10 hours. Cook before serving.

Hot-Smoked Flounder

- Fillet the fish. Remove the skin.
- Brine the 1/2" fillets for 5 minutes in 80° brine. Wash and drain.
- Dry fillets for 60 minutes in a smokehouse preheated to 100° F (38° C).
- Smoke for 60 minutes at 185° F (85° C). Switch off the heat and smoke for 15 minutes more.
- Cool in air.

Flounder Avocado Cocktail

2 cups flaked flounder
1 cup cocktail sauce
1 cup avocado cubes
Parsley
Lemon wedges

Cocktail sauce

3/4 cup catsup
1/4 cup lemon juice
1/4 tsp salt
6 drops tabasco sauce
3 Tbsp finely chopped celery

Combine all ingredients and chill.
Arrange layers of cocktail sauce, avocado and fish in cocktail glasses.
Begin and end with cocktail sauce.
Garnish with parsley and lemon wedges.

Haddock *(Melanogrammus aeglefinus)*

Name	Protein %	Fat %	Water %
Haddock	16.32	0.45	83.38

The name haddock is used in Britain to describe only one species, *Melanogrammus aeglefinus*, and there are no other English common names for it. The vast majority of haddocks landed in Britain are between 30 and 70 cm. The haddock feeds mainly on shellfish, sea urchins, worms, and small fish like sand eels and capelin. The haddock is found on both sides of the north Atlantic but is more abundant on the European side. The chemical composition of haddock flesh is similar to that of cod and other members of the cod family.

Single fillets are taken from large haddocks, but most small haddocks are block filleted, for sale fresh or frozen, or for making golden cutlets. *A block fillet* is the flesh cut from both sides of the fish, *the two pieces remaining joined along the back.* The fillets may be marketed with or without skin, but the skin with its distinctive 'thumbprint' is often left on the fillet to enable the buyer to distinguish the haddock from less valuable species. Increasing amounts of small haddock fillets are used for the manufacture of laminated blocks, that is frozen blocks of skinless, boneless fillets which can be cut into pieces of uniform size and weight for sale as fish fingers or portions.

The haddock is used to make a number of smoked white fish products, notably the finnan haddock and similar cured products, the golden cutlet and smoked single fillet, all of which are cold smoked, and the *smokie, which is hot smoked.*

English seaport of Grimsby has been famous for smoked haddock. The UK's Department for Environment, Food and Rural Affairs (DEFRA), defines Traditional Grimsby smoked fish "as fillets of cod and haddock, weighing between 200 and 700 grams, which have been cold smoked in accordance with the traditional method and within a defined geographical area around Grimsby. In 2009, Traditional Grimsby smoked fish was awarded Protected Geographical Indication (PGI) status by the European Commission.

Finnan Haddock

The finnan haddock, or finnan, is made by beheading a medium sized gutted haddock, cleaning the gut cavity by removing the black skin and any traces of blood and kidney lying beneath the backbone, and then splitting the fish open by cutting along the underside from neck to tail; in the so-called London cut the backbone lies on the left side of the split fish, whereas in the Aberdeen cut the backbone is on the right.

The split fish are brined for 7-15 minutes in an 80° brine, depending on size; for example a haddock 16" (40 cm) long and weighing about 18 oz (½ kg) requires about 10 minutes. No dye is added to the brine.

The brined fish are either tentered or speated, and left to drain for a time so that a good surface gloss develops. The fish are smoked at 80° F (27° C); a ½ kg fish takes about 3½ hours in a mechanical kiln, but smaller fish may take only 3 hours, whereas large haddock may take 4 hours or more to attain the desired pale straw color.

Photo 6.17a Finnan haddock fillet.

Golden Cutlets *(block fillets)*

The golden cutlet is made from a block fillet of haddock or whiting. The fillet is brined for about 3 minutes in 80° brine, laid over banjoes or tentered by the tail, left to drain and to develop a gloss on the cut surface for about 2 hours and then smoked at 80° F (27° C); cutlets take 2-2½ hours in a mechanical kiln. A small amount of dye is usually added to the brine bath.

Glasgow Pales

The pales are made mainly from small haddock, less than 0.75 lb, and they are smoked so lightly that they have only the barest detectable smoky flavour and almost no yellow color. The fish are beheaded, cleaned and split along the belly so that the backbone remains on the left side of the fish. Fish are brined in 80° brine for 4-5 minutes, drained and smoked at 80° F (27° C) for 2.5 hours.

Smoked Fillet

Single fillets with the skin on, taken from medium and large haddocks, are brined for 4-10 minutes depending on size in 80° brine to which dye may be added, laid over screens and drained for at least 2 hours, and then smoked at 80° F (27° C) for 5 hours. The skin is left on not only to distinguish smoked haddock from smoked cod, but also to prevent the softer flesh of the haddock from gaping and tearing too much.

Smokies

Smokies are hot smoked small haddocks. The fish are beheaded and the gut cavity cleaned out. Gutted haddocks weighing 0.5 - 0.75 lb are selected. The first smokies were made in Arbroath, south of Aberdeen in Scotland. The smoked haddocks were called smokies due to their dark tarry appearance which was the result of smoking in a barrel over a fire. The fish are tied together by the tail in pairs and brined for 30-45 minutes in 80° brine.

The brined haddocks are hung over smokesticks and:

- smoked at 176 - 194° F (80-90° C) for 1 hour. This dries out the skin and will help to obtain golden brown color.
- smoked at 110 - 120° F (43 - 49° C) for 1 hour.
- cooked with smoke at 160 - 170° F (72 - 77° C) for 1 hour.

The finished product can be eaten without further cooking.

Halibut

Name	Protein %	Fat %	Water %
Halibut, Atlantic & Pacific	18.56	1.33	80.34
Halibut, Greenland	14.37	13.84	70.27

The halibut is the largest flat fish and range in size from 5 to 400 pounds and grow to over 8 feet long. All flat fish are opportunistic bottom dwellers that will swallow any suitable food. Flounder can be found in cold, temperate and even tropical waters, however, halibut prefer cold water temperatures ranging from 37 - 46° F (3 - 8° C).

Photo 6.17 Halibut caught off Raspberry Island, Alaska.

Author: NancyHeise at en.wikipedia

Smoked Halibut

Fillet the fish. Rinse.
Immerse in 80° brine for 10 minutes. Rinse and drain.
Air dry for 1 hour.

Apply a light smoke at 100° F (38° C) for 30 minutes.
Increase the temperature to 212° F (100° C) and smoke with medium
dense smoke for 120 minutes.

Halibut Jellied Pineapple Salad

2 cups flaked smoked halibut
1 can (1 pound 4 ounces) crushed pineapple
2 packages lime flavored gelatin
1-1/2 cups boiling water
2 cups pineapple juice and water
1/4 cup lemon juice
1 teaspoon salt
1/2 cup silvered toasted almonds
1/2 cup mayonnaise or salad dressing
1 teaspoon lemon juice

Drain pineapple and save liquid.
Dissolve gelatin in boiling water.
Add pineapple juice and water, lemon juice and salt.
Place in a 1-quart ring mold; chill until firm.
Combine almonds, mayonnaise, lemon juice, salt, pineapple and fish.
Chill.
Unmold gelatin on salad greens and fill center with fish mixture.
Garnish with radishes.

Halibut Jellied Salad

2 cups flaked smoked halibut
1 package lemon flavored gelatin
1-1/2 cups boiling water
1/4 cup vinegar
1/2 teaspoon salt
1 cup grated carrot
1/4 cup chopped green pepper
Lettuce
Mayonnaise or salad dressing

Dissolve gelatin in boiling water.
Add vinegar and salt; chill until almost congealed.
Fold in carrot, green pepper and fish.
Place in 6 individual molds; chill until firm.
Unmold on lettuce; garnish with mayonnaise.

Herring

Name	Protein %	Fat %	Water %
Herring, Atlantic	17.96	9.04	72.05
Herring, Pacific	16.39	13.88	71.52

The most abundant and commercially important species belong to the genus Clupea, found particularly in shallow, temperate waters of the North Pacific *(Clupea pallasii)* and the North Atlantic oceans, including the Baltic Sea *(Clupea harengus)*, as well as off the west coast of South America (Chile).

Photo 6.18 Skipjack herring.

Creator: Raver, Duane.
U.S. Fish and Wildlife Service

The average size of herring is between 9-12" (23-30 cm). The body is covered with large, thin, loosely attached scales. Unlike most white fish, the chemical composition of herring varies considerably with the season and the breeding cycle; the fat content of herring may be less than 1 per cent immediately after spawning, and more than 20 per cent as spawning time approaches again. Herring is one of the most popular fish in northern European countries.

It is produced in oil, sour cream, sour cream and beets, it is smoked, and canned in many different ways.

- **Kippers** - the kipper and the kipper fillet are the most important smoked products made from herring in Britain.

- **Bloaters** - are whole ungutted herring, dry salted for about 6 hours and cold smoked for 8-12 hours in a traditional chimney kiln or 4 hours in a mechanical kiln; the fish are dried without smoke for most of the time in the kiln, and smoke is applied only during the last hour or so, so that the fish retain their bright silver appearance.

- **Buckling** - are hot smoked herring; the flesh is cooked during the smoking process. In British practice the herring are nobbed, that is the head and long gut are removed, brined, and smoked for about 3 hours in a mechanical kiln, the temperature being raised gradually from about 86° F, (30° C) at the start to 167° F (75° C) during the last hour.

- **Red herring** - are whole ungutted herring that have been heavily salted and then cold smoked for 2-3 weeks; the hard cured product is exported, mainly to Mediterranean countries.

Kippers

A kipper is a fat herring with guts and gills removed, split down the back from head to tail, lightly brined, dyed if desired, and cold smoked. All herring, whether chilled or thawed after cold storage, should first be washed to remove loose scales and other debris. The herring is laid on the filleting bench with the back of the fish facing the operator. The blade of a small kippering knife is inserted at the centre of the back of the head and a cut made through the skull to the mouth. The knife is again inserted at the same entry point and a second deep cut is made down to the tail, keeping the blade of the knife close enough to the backbone to leave just a thin layer of flesh over it. The herring is then opened so that the backbone is on the left side of the kipper, gills and guts are removed, and the backbone trimmed where necessary with the knife. The split herring is then washed before brining. The brining time for kippers depends mainly upon the size of the fish and the fat content; the salt content of the finished product should be between 1-8 and 2-5 percent to suit the average palate.

Kippers	Time in 80° brine
Small winter herring	10 minutes
Medium-size fat herring	15 minutes
Large herring	20 minutes
Very large herring	30 minutes

Kippers were smoked in mechanical kiln for 4 hours. In home smokers smoke for 6 hours at 86° F (30° C) or lower. The estimated weight loss is about 14%.

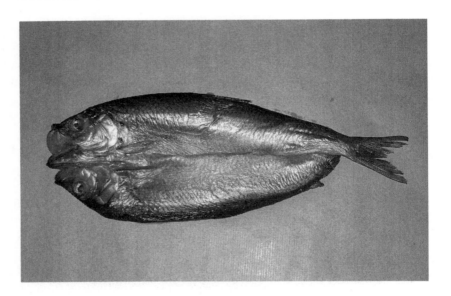

Photo 6.19 Kipper.

Gaius Cornelius-Wikimedia Commons.

Making Kipper Fillets

Kipper fillets are prepared either by cutting block fillets, smoking them and then cutting single fillets from them, or by cutting single fillets from the raw herring and smoking them. Block fillets are taken by making a transverse cut across the back of the head of the herring, and then cutting down towards the belly wall and in towards the backbone, continuing the cut to the tail so that the flesh on one side of the fish is separated from the bone. Care must be taken not to penetrate the belly wall. The cut is repeated on the other side of the fish, so that the *double fillet, joined by the skin and back fins, can be removed from the head and skeleton in one piece.* The tail fin is left on if the block fillets are to be tentered.

Kipper fillets	Time in 80° brine
Medium-size	3-4 minutes
Large fillets	6-8 minutes

Kipper fillets are smoked for 2½-3 hours in a mechanical kiln, depending on size, and should lose 10-12 per cent of their brined weight. The temperature in the kiln should not rise above 85° F (30° C). Kipper fillets may take 4-8 hours in a traditional smokehouses.

Bloaters

Bloaters are made from whole, ungutted and slightly salted herring. They owe their characteristic flavor, to the enzymes or ferments from the gut. The fish are salted and left overnight. After salting the fish are washed and threaded on speats through the gills and mouth or through the eyes. The fish are processed as follows:

- Drying (no smoke or very thin smoke) at 185 - 194° F (85 - 90° C) for 3 hours.
- Smoking at 185 - 194° F (85 - 90° C) for 1 hour.

As a result, the fish develops little color and and a faint smoky flavor.

Buckling *(Herring)*

Buckling, originally a German product, very popular on the continent is a *hot smoked herring*. There is not a standard form of fish preparation. The fish can be beheaded or not, also, the gut may or may not be removed.

1. In Britain, *nobbing* the herring was the preferred method - the whole herring is beheaded and the gut pulled out, leaving any roe or milt in position.

2. The fish are cured in 80° brine for 60 minutes, briefly rinsed and hung on speats. The speat is pushed through the thick part of the flesh near the shoulder. The fish are drained and let to dry until they don't drip water anymore.

3. Herring are placed in smokehouse (it is customary to smoke them when still wet to obtain a golden brown color) and they are:

- smoked at 80-90° F (27-32° C) for 1 hour. This dries out the skin and will help to obtain golden brown color.
- smoked at 110 - 120° F (43 - 49° C) for 1 hour.
- cooked with smoke at 160 - 170° F (72 - 77° C) for 1 hour.

Red Herring

Red herring was a popular product in England and Netherlands as it had en excellent keeping properties. The fish was well mixed with salt, taking about 30% salt to 100% of the fish (by weight). The fish was not gutted. Then the fish were placed in barrels and cured forr 3 days to even 6 weeks. Then the fish were desalted in water, drained and dried from 12 to 24 hours. After that the fish were smoked from 3 to 6 weeks at about 65° F (18° C). The finished product had a very long shelf life and was exported to counties with warmer climate.

Mackerel - Atlantic *(Scomber scombrus)*

Name	Protein %	Fat %	Water %
Mackerel, Atlantic	18.60	13.89	63.55
Mackerel, Spanish	19.29	6.30	71.67

Scomber scombrus is sometimes called Atlantic, northern or Boston mackerel to distinguish it from *Scomber japonicus*, which is variously called chub, Pacific, or Spanish mackerel.

The back of the Atlantic mackerel is a brilliant greenish blue, and the head is a steely blue-black with a small yellow patch behind the eye. There are 23-33 dark wavy bands across the back of the fish down to the midline. The sides have a silvery or coppery sheen, the belly is silvery white and there is a broken black line just below the lateral line. The scales are small and the skin feels velvety. An adult mackerel 30-35 cm long weighs 300-500 g before gutting.

The mackerel is a fatty fish, and the fat and water content vary with season. The fat content of mackerel caught off south west England is lowest in May after spawning, and reaches its peak between October and December after the fish have fed during the summer and autumn. A typical range of fat content throughout the year is 6-23 per cent. As fat content increases, water content decreases; the typical range of water content is 56-74 percent. The protein content is 18-20 percent.

Photo 6.20 Atlantic mackerel.

Gutted mackerel may be split down the back in the same way as herring are prepared for kippering. A split mackerel of average size and fat content requires 7 minutes in 80° brine. The fish may also be cut as single or block fillets; brining time is 3 minutes in 80° brine.

Hot Smoked Atlantic Mackerel

1. Wash the fish, cut the head off, split the belly and remove the entrails. Use a brush to scrape off kidneys. Rinse and drain.

2. Brine the fish for 10 minutes in 80° brine. Rinse and drain. Insert on rods (Photo 4.9).
3. Dry fish for 60 minutes in a preheated to 100° F (38° C) smokehouse. Light smoke is allowed.
4. Apply a dense smoke for 60 minutes at 185° F (85° C). Switch off the heat and smoke for 15 more minutes.

Mackerel - Spanish (*Scomberomorus maculatus*)

The Spanish mackerel prefers warm waters and is a common fish in Florida. It looks similar to the Atlantic mackerel, but is bigger and instead of wavy bands, there are large dots on its sides.

Photo 6.21 Spanish mackerel has dotted body.

Hot Smoked Spanish Mackerel

1. Fillet the fish. Leave the skin on.

Photo 6.22 Spanish mackerel fillet.

2. Brine fillets for 5 minutes in 80° brine. Wash and drain.

Photo 6.23 Brining fillets in 80° brine.

3. Air dry fillets for 60 minutes.

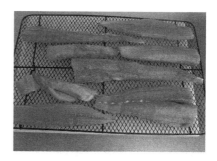

Photo 6.24 Drying fillets for best skin gloss.

4. Insert into a smokehouse preheated to 100° F (38° C) and apply a light smoke for 60 minutes.

5. Apply a dense smoke for 60-90 minutes at 185° F (85° C).

King Mackerel *(Scomberomorus cavalla)*

Name	Protein %	Fat %	Water %
King mackerel	20.28	2	78.55

The king mackerel is a migratory species of mackerel of the western Atlantic Ocean and Gulf of Mexico. The king mackerel is a medium-sized fish, typically encountered from five to 30 pounds, but is known to exceed 90 pounds. Fish under 10 pounds (5 kg) show yellowish-brown spots on the flanks, somewhat smaller than the spots of the Atlantic Spanish mackerel. They may be sold as fillets, steaks, or in the round (whole). Their raw flesh is grayish, due to its high fat content. They are best prepared by broiling, frying, baking or, especially for large "smoker" king, by smoking.

Photo 6.25 Spanish mackerel left, King mackerel right.

Smoked King Mackerel

Fillet the fish. Rinse.
Immerse in 80° brine for 10 minutes. Rinse and drain.
Air dry for 1 hour.
Apply a light smoke at 100° F (38° C) for 60 minutes.
Apply a dense smoke for 90 minutes at 185° F (85° C).

Mackerel Pate

A delicious pate can be made from the flesh of hot smoked mackerel, either on a commercial scale or in small quantities for domestic use. The flesh is taken off the whole smoked fish, and all bones are carefully removed. For commercial production this can be done satisfactorily in a mechanical separator.

The flesh is mixed with softened or melted butter in a high speed blender, using 7 parts by weight of fish to 3 parts of butter. When the mixture is of smooth consistency, flavouring or spices may be added if required; for example lemon juice and pepper can be used. Manufacturers can readily devise their own variations on the basic recipe. Some white fish flesh is sometimes added to compensate for variations in the fat content of the mackerel flesh in the mix. The product is not sterile, and should not be kept more than 1 day at ambient temperature, or more than 5 days at 32-35° F (0-2° C). The pate can be frozen and cold stored in suitable containers.

Mackerel Deviled Spread

10 oz smoked mackerel flakes
4 oz cream
4 oz Philadelphia cream cheese
1 Tbsp lemon juice
1/2 tsp pepper
1/2 tsp tabasco sauce

Whip cream, add cream cheese and blend together. Add lemon juice, pepper, smoked mackerel and blend together. Chill.

Mackerel Horseradish Spread

8 oz smoked mackerel
3 oz butter
4 Tbsp double cream
1 Tbsp creamed horseradish
1/2 tsp pepper
1 dash cayenne pepper
1 lemon grated zest
Fresh parsley to garnish

Run all ingredients in food processor. Chill. Decorate with parsley before serving.

Mullet *(Mugil cephalus)*

Name	Protein %	Fat %	Water %
Mullet	19.35	3.79	77.01

As mullet is most abundant in the Gulf of Mexico and the Caribbean sea, we may assume that this is where the most fish will be smoked. The climate is hot there so the hot smoking method will be applied, although one can cold smoke fish at night hours in December, January and February.

Photo 6.26 Mullet.

Mullet are a coastal species that have an affinity for tropical and warm temperate waters. Many consider the Gulf of Mexico to be mullet country, and of course they are everywhere in West Florida. They can be seen jumping out of the water. However, they can be found throughout the entire east coast of the United States reaching Nova Scotia, Canada, and on the west coast of the United States from Southern California down to Chile, the coast of Brazil, the Mediterranean Sea, the Black Sea, the coast of France, around the entire coast of Africa, Taiwan, and in Australia.

As the water temperature rises in the summer months, mullet wander into and are more abundant in brackish and freshwater. Mullet are able to tolerate wide salinity and temperature levels of water and those characteristics allow the fish to prosper in many areas of the world.

There are two common types of mullet found throughout the Gulf of Mexico. The silver mullet and the striped mullet. The striped mullet is a larger fish ranging from around 1 to 2 feet and the silver mullet measures up to one foot.

Mullet are vegetarians that eat detritus, which is disintegrated material found at the bottom. It is almost futile to catch mullet with a fishing rod. To catch mullet you need a cast net.

Photo 6.27 Although the net fits into a common plastic bucket it spreads 14 feet in diameter when thrown. Throwing net requires some practice. You can find all about the technique in the book: *"The Amazing Mullet."*

Casting net is not just the skill, it is the art.

Photo 6.28 Adam Marianski casting net in St.Petersburg, Florida.

Photo 6.29 The net sinks.

Photo 6.30 Casting net is legal in Florida.

Photo 6.31 The old St.Petersburg pier in the background.

Photo 6.32 A catch of mullet. On a lucky full moon throw you can get 50 or more mullet. There is a bonus: you get other fish, including crabs.

Smoking Mullet

Mullet is semi-fat fish which is great when smoked. The fish is very easy to clean and is usually smoked "butterfly" style.

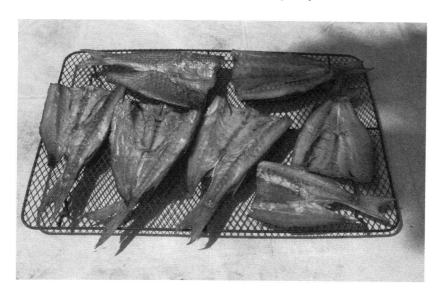

Photo 6.33 Smoked mullet.

Cold Smoked Mullet

Split mullet (see Chapter 2). Wash well and drain.
Dredge in salt, and pack in a container, cover with salt. Salt for 2 hours. Rinse and place on wire screens. Air dry for 2 hours.
Cold smoke at <80° F (27° C) for 12 hours with light smoke. Apply medium dense smoke and smoke for 12 hours more (total smoking time 24 hours).

Hot Smoked Mullet

Split mullet (see Chapter 2).
Immerse for 10 minutes in 80° brine.
Rinse well and drain. Air dry for 1 hour.
Smoke with a light smoke at 100° F (38° C) for 60 minutes.
Smoke with a dense smoke at 176° F (80° C) for 90 minutes.

A great variety of spreads, pastes and dips are made with smoked mullet. Mix about 50% of smoked mullet with other ingredients of your choice.

Mullet Avocado Spread

Smoked mullet	8 oz. (225 g)
Avocado	2 (about 400 g total)
Lemon juice	3 Tbsp.
Vegetable oil	1 Tbsp.
Double cream	2 Tbsp.
Garlic, smashed	1 clove
Salt and pepper to taste	

Place smoked mullet trimmings, lemon juice and oil in blender and mix. Add double cream, garlic, salt and pepper and mix again until smooth.

Mullet Curry Spread

Smoked mullet	8 oz. (225 g)
Lemon juice	2 Tbsp.
Plain yogurt	8 Tbsp. (2 oz., 56 g)
Mayonnaise	2 Tbsp.
Curry powder	1 tsp.

Place smoked mullet trimmings and lemon juice in food processor and mix. Add yogurt, mayonnaise, curry powder and process until smooth.

Mullet Cream Cheese

Smoked mullet	8 oz. (225 g)
Philadelphia cream cheese	4 oz. (113 g)
Softened butter	1 oz. (28 g)
Lemon juice	2 Tbsp.
Mayonnaise	4 Tbsp.
Sherry wine	1 Tbsp.
White pepper	½ tsp.
Nutmeg	⅓ tsp.

Place smoked mullet trimmings, lemon juice and sherry in blender and mix. Add cream cheese, butter, mayonnaise, pepper and nutmeg and mix again until smooth.

Mullet Dip

Smoked mullet	8 oz. (225 g)
Sour cream	1 cup
Mayonnaise	½ cup
Scallions, finely chopped	1 Tbsp.
Lemon juice	1 Tbsp.
Tabasco sauce	3-4 drops
Worcestershire sauce	1/4 tsp.

Chop smoked mullet trimmings, sour cream, mayonnaise and lemon juice in food processor. Add other ingredients and process until smooth. Cover and refrigerate. Serve with potato chips or crackers.

Mullet Guacamole Spread

Guacamole is a popular avocado based dip which originated in Mexico. Authentic guacamole is made with avocado, tomato, cumin, cilantro, and lime juice.

Smoked mullet	8 oz (225 g)
Avocado	2 fruits (about 400 g total)
Lime or lemon juice	4 Tbsp.
Cilantro, chopped	2 Tbsp.
Medium Size Tomato (Roma), diced	1 tomato (80 g)
Ground cumin	⅓ tsp.
Medium onion, diced	1 (about 90 g)
Garlic clove, minced	1
Cayenne	⅓ tsp.
White pepper (to taste)	about ¼ tsp.
Salt (to taste)	about ¼ tsp.

1. Cut the avocados lengthways and scoop out avocado pulp.
2. Chop smoked mullet trimmings with lemon juice in food processor.
3. Add avocado pulp and all other ingredients. Process until smooth.

Photo 6.34 Horseradish spread.

Mullet Horseradish Spread

Smoked mullet	8 oz. (225 g)
Softened butter	2 oz. (56 g)
Lemon juice	2 Tbsp.
Plain yogurt	4 Tbsp.
Creamed horseradish	2 Tbsp.
Salt	½ tsp
White pepper	½ tsp

In a food processor mix smoked mullet trimmings and lemon juice. Add yogurt, butter, creamed horseradish and process until smooth.

Mullet Mousse

Smoked mullet	8 oz. (225 g)
Softened butter	2 oz. (56 g)
Lemon juice	2 Tbsp.
Vegetable oil	1 Tbsp.
Cayenne	⅓ tsp.
Double cream	8 Tbsp. (¼ cup)
Mayonnaise	2 Tbsp.
Egg white	1

Place smoked mullet trimmings, oil and lemon juice in food processor and chop in processor until smooth. Add double cream, mayonnaise, butter, cayenne and process again. In a separate bowl whip egg white. Add egg white and mix everything well again.

Mullet Soft Spread

Smoked mullet	8 oz. (225 g)
Sour cream	4 oz. (112 g)
Mayonnaise	2 Tbsp.
Heavy cream	2 Tbsp.
Lemon juice	1 Tbsp.
Onion powder	1 tsp.
Chives, finely chopped	1 Tbsp.
White pepper	½ tsp.
Salt	½ tsp.

Place smoked mullet trimmings, heavy cream and lemon juice in food processor and mix. Add sour cream, mayonnaise and all other ingredients and process until smooth. Chives may be replaced with dill.

Perch *(Morone americana)*

Perch is a small fish, common in Florida waters. It has a tough lower jaw area and there is a limited amount of space between the vent and jaw for gutting. The easiest approach is to cut off the head and then to gut the fish.

Photo 6.35 White perch.

Smoked Perch

Scale the fish. Cut off the head, split the belly from the vent until the hard bony structure of the jaw. Remove the entrails.
Wash the cavity and the fish.
Brine for 5 minutes in 80° brine.
Wash and drain.
Dry the fish for 60 minutes in a preheated to 100° F (38° C) smokehouse.
Smoke for 60 minutes at 185° F (85° C). Switch off the heat and smoke for 30 minutes more.

Photo 6.36 Perch.

Red Drum *(Sciaenops ocellatus)*

The red drum, also known as channel bass, red fish, spot tail bass or simply reds, is a game fish that is found in the Atlantic Ocean from Massachusetts to Florida and in the Gulf of Mexico from Florida to Northern Mexico. At the age of 3-4 years the red fish is mature fish about 30 inches long and 4 kg (8.8 lb) in weight. As red drum grow longer, they increase in weight and size. Red fish may have red colored body but its meat is white and delicious when cooked, however, to enjoy the fish, you have to catch the fish yourself. They may no longer be commercially harvested in U.S. federal waters or in most state waters. Commercial netting disappeared after coastal states like Florida declared red drum prohibited for sale.

Photo 6.37 Captain Brian Mitchell holding red drum, Treasure Island, Florida. The most distinguishing mark on the red drum is a large black spot on the upper part of the tail base.

Red drum are a red color on the back, which fades into white on the belly. The fish is called the red "drum" because they make a drumming sound when distressed.

Red drum is good for eating. It is a big meaty fish that offers large fillets.

Photo 6.38 Red drum.

Smoked Red Drum

Fillet the fish. Rinse.
Immerse in 80° brine for 10 minutes. Rinse and drain.
Air dry for 1 hour.
Apply a light smoke at 100° F (38° C) for 30 minutes.
Increase the temperature to 185° F (85° C) and smoke with medium smoke for 120 minutes.

Salmon

Name	Protein %	Fat %	Water %
Salmon, Pink	20.50	4.40	75.52
Salmon, Chum	20.14	3.77	75.38
Salmon, Chinook	19.93	10.43	71.64
Salmon, Sockeye	21.31	5.61	73.15
Salmon, Coho	21.62	5.93	72.66
Salmon, Coho, farmed	21.27	7.67	70.47
Salmon, Atlantic	19.84	6.34	68.50
Salmon, Atlantic, farmed	20.42	13.42	64.89

Salmon is the common name for several species of fish in the family *Salmonidae*. Other fish in the same family are called trout. All types of salmon contain a large percentage of fat, and that is why smoked salmon is so delicious.

Photo 6.39 King salmon.

Image donated by Doug Alcorn. Gulkana River, Sourdough, Alaska.
U.S. Fish and Wildlife Service

There is Atlantic salmon, Pacific salmon, Australian salmon, Hawaiian salmon, Indian salmon, Danube European salmon, the fish can be found everywhere. The size varies with species and can range from 50 cm, 6.8 kg for pink and Sockeye salmon to 120 cm, 46.8 kg for Atlantic salmon.

General Guidelines

All salmon species are suitable for smoking. The whole fish should be carefully gutted and the belly cavity cleaned out. The contents of the belly cavity can constitute up to 25 percent of the weight of the fish as caught. Congealed blood in and around the main vein along the backbone should be removed; a large spoon is often suitable for this purpose. The belly cavity should then be well washed.

After gutting, the head is removed by cutting round inside the gills, then breaking or cutting through the backbone. Two single fillets, are cut, each complete with nape or shoulder bone, and belly flap. The nape bone gives strength to the fillet during handling, and provides support *if the fillet is to be hung for smoking*, although most fillets nowadays are smoked on trays. The belly bones and covering membrane can be carefully removed from each fillet to enhance appearance, although some smokers prefer to leave them on. As much blood as possible is removed from veins by pressing them gently inwards, and any blood on the surface of the fillet is wiped away with cold water; blood left on the fillet becomes black and unattractive in appearance when the fillet is smoked.

Cold Smoked Salmon

The whole salmon are gutted; the fish are beheaded and filleted. The lug bones are left on fillets to provide strong support for the hanging loop, although most fillets nowadays are smoked on trays. String is threaded through the shoulder of each fillet under the lug bones to form a loop. The lug bones are not needed when the fillets are lied down on a screen.

Salt can be added to salmon fillets either by brining or by dry salting. Brining may give a better gloss, but almost all producers prefer dry salting because subsequent drying/smoking time in the smokehouse is shorter. Brined fillets, which *lose no weight during brining*, need about *twice as long* in the smokehouse to give the same total weight loss.

To allow the salt to penetrate the fillet more evenly, the skin can be scorched at the thickest part of the fillet with a razor blade without cutting the meat. Three cuts are made that just penetrate the skin on the fillet, each about 2" long across the width of the fillet at the thickest part to allow uniform salt penetration, the slits being packed with salt. The fillets are placed on a layer of salt 1 inch thick. The cut side of the fillet is covered with another layer of salt about 1/2 inch deep at the thick end tapering down to the tail. At the thinnest part of the tail the salt is only lightly sprinkled over.

Additional alternate layers of fillets and salt can be laid on top of the first layer until the stack is complete. Typical times in practice are about 12 hours for fillets from a 4 kg salmon, and 24 hours for fillets from an 8 kg salmon, but the time will vary to some extent depending on initial quality and fat content. *The accumulating pickle should be drained away.*

Note: There are cures that include small amounts of brown sugar, molasses and rum to introduce a distinctive flavour, but the majority of producers use only salt.

Salting times:

- 1.5 - 2 lb fillet (0.75 inch) - 12 hours
- 3 - 4 lb fillet (1 inch) - 16 hours
- 5 lb fillet (1.5 inch) - 24 hours

By this stage the fillets should feel firm and springy, rather like bacon, when pressed with the fingers, having lost the stiffness they had when taken out of dry salt. The salmon fillets, are either hung on (enters by means of string loops through the shoulders or are laid on trays made of plastics coated or stainless steel wire mesh. Hanging has the disadvantage that it tends to stretch a heavy fillet and cause its flesh to gape (separate).

Salted fillets are washed in cold water to remove surplus salt from the surface and then immersed in 30° brine for 1/2 hour depending on size to even out the salt distribution. The fillets are hung up to drip.

The fillets are dried at 80° F (27° C) in a smokehouse (no smoke needed) for 4 hours.

The fillets are smoked with thin smoke at 80° F (27° C) for 12 hours.

In the last 20 minutes of smoking the temperature may be raised for 20 minutes to 92° F (33° C) to bring oil to the surface which gives fillets an attractive appearance. If fillets on removal from the smokehouse are found to be too soft and flabby, they should be returned to the smokehouse and dried more. The finished product should have a consistency rather like that of boiled ham, not too dry and fibrous, and be easily sliced. The shelf life of refrigerated smoked salmon is 5-6 days.

Medium cured salmon should loose 7-9% of weight during dry salting and additional 7-9% during smoking; a combined weight loss of 16-18%.

Salmon - Nova Lox - Cold Smoked

Mix one part brown sugar with one part of salt.
The fillets are placed skin down on a layer of salt/sugar about 1 inch thick.
Thoroughly cover fillets with the mixture on top.
Add more layers in the same manner, place the last fillets skin up and cover with more mix.

Salting times:

- 0.75 inch - 9 hours

- 1 inch - 12 hours

- 1.5 inch - 18 hours

- 2 inch - 24 hours

Rinse fillets to remove surplus salt from the surface and drain.

Now, immerse fillets in 80° brine.

Place fillets in cold water: thin fillets - 60 minutes, thick fillets - 120 minutes. Change water 1-2 times. Drain.
Dry at < 80° F (26° C) for 60 minutes.
Smoke with a thin smoke at < 80° F (26° C) for 12 - 16 hours.

Cold Smoked Salmon

This recipe uses 2:1 salt to brown sugar.

Make 80° brine first, then add brown sugar. For example, to 1 gallon of water you will add 2.2 pounds of salt and 1.1 pound of brown sugar. The solution is denser now, and will show as 95° brine on salinometer. If you like spices, for example dill or bay leaf, add them now.

Place fillets in the brine.

Brining times:

- 0.75 inch - 9 hours
- 1 inch - 12 hours
- 1.5 inch - 18 hours
- 2 inch - 24 hours

Place fillets in cold water: thin fillets - 60 minutes, thick fillets - 120 minutes. Change water 1-2 times. Drain.
Place in refrigerator for 12 hours. Salt will equalize inside fillets and their surfaces will dry.
Smoke at 70° F (22° C) for 12 - 16 hours, depending on size.

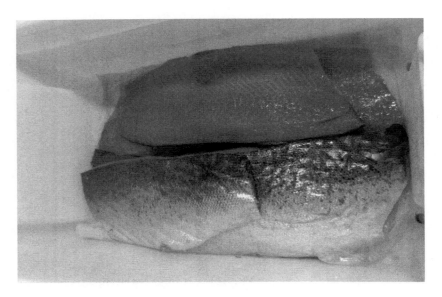

Photo 6.40 Smoked salmon fillets.

Hot Smoked Salmon

Place salmon fillets for 1 - 2 hours in 80 degrees brine:

- 0.75 inch - 30 min
- 1 inch - 60 minutes
- 1.5 inch - 90 minutes
- 2 inch - 120 minutes

Remove the fish from the brine and rinse it quickly under cold running water. Drain.

Rub screens with a cloth soaked with vegetable oil.

Place the screens in smokehouse preheated to 100° F (38° C) for 1 hour.

Start smoking at 100° F (38° C) for 60 minutes. Increase the temperature to 176° F (80° C).

Smoke at 176° F (80° C) for 60 minutes. Thick fillets may need more time.

Cool to room temperature.

Note: you can use sugar brine (see Cold Smoked Salmon above).

Salmon a la King

1-pound can salmon
1/3 cup green pepper, chopped
1 teaspoon onion, grated
1/4 cup pimiento, chopped
1/4 cup butter or other fat, melted
1/4 cup flour
1 teaspoon salt

Dash pepper
2 cups milk
2 egg yolks, beaten
1 4-ounce can mushrooms, drained and sliced
Toast cups, patty shells, or toast

Drain and flake salmon.

Cook green pepper, onion and pimiento in butter until tender.

Blend in flour and seasonings.

Add milk and cook until thick and smooth, stirring constantly.

Stir a little of the hot sauce into the beaten egg yolks and add to the sauce, stirring constantly.

Add salmon and mushrooms; heat thoroughly.

Serve in toast cups, patty shells or on toast.

Salmon Bechamel

1-pound can salmon
3 tablespoons butter or other fat
1/4 cup flour
1/2 teaspoon salt
Dash pepper
Dash nutmeg
2 cups liquid (liquid from canned salmon plus milk to make volume)
2 hard boiled eggs, chopped
3 cups cooked rice

Drain and flake salmon, saving liquid.
Melt butter and blend in flour and seasonings.
Add liquid gradually and cook until thick and smooth, stirring constantly.
Add salmon and eggs; heat.
Serve over rice or in a rice ring.

Salmon Canapes

1 7-ounce can smoked salmon
1 3-ounce package cream cheese
2 tablespoons mayonnaise or salad dressing
1/2 cup celery, finely diced
1/4 teaspoon salt
1/4 teaspoon prepared mustard
16 slices bread

Drain fish and grind twice.
Cream the cheese and mayonnaise.
Blend in fish, celery and seasonings.
Remove crusts from bread.
Cut each slice into 3 strips and toast.
Spread salmon on toast strips and garnish.

Salmon Club Sandwich

1-pound can salmon
3 tablespoons celery, chopped
3 tablespoons weet pickle, chopped
3 tablespoons onion, chopped
1/2 cup mayonnaise or salad dressing
18 slices buttered bread
4 tomatoes, sliced
12 lettuce leaves

Drain and flake salmon.
Combine with celery, sweet pickle, onion and mayonnaise.
Spread six slices of bread with fix mixture; cover each with a second slice of bread and place tomatoes and lettuce on each; cover with the remaining six slices of bread.
Fasten sandwiches with toothpicks.
Cut into quarters.
Garnish and serve.

Salmon Cream Cheese

Chopped or ground salmon trimmings 125 g (4.4 oz)
Cream cheese 125 g (4.4 oz)
Clear consomme 125 ml (½ cup)
Salt, pepper, lemon juice to taste
Chopped parsley or dill for decoration
Mix warm consomme with cream cheese.
Add seasonings, chopped salmon and mix everything together.
Place in refrigerator and when set, sprinkle with parsley or dill.

Salmon Dip

125 g (4.4 oz) finely chopped or ground salmon trimmings
75 ml (2 fl. oz) heavy cream
30 ml (1 oz) single cream
15 ml (1 Tbsp) lemon juice
15 ml (1 Tbsp) vegetable oil
1 tsp dried dill
Salt, pepper, pinch of cayenne to taste

In a food processor blend single cream, lemon juice and oil.
Add other ingredients and chopped salmon and blend together.
Place in containers and refrigerate.

Salmon Salad

1-pound can salmon
1/2 cup mayonnaise or salad dressing
1/2 cup celery, chopped
1/2 cup cooked peas
2 tablespoons sweet pickle, chopped
2 tablespoons onion, chopped
3 hard boiled eggs, chopped
Lettuce

Drain and flake salmon.
Combine all ingredients except lettuce, being careful not to break the
fish into too small pieces.
Serve in lettuce cups and garnish.

Salmon Stuffed Tomatoes Salad

1 7-ounce can smoked salmon
2 hard boiled eggs, chopped
3/4 cup celery, chopped
1/4 cup cucumber, chopped
1 tablespoon onion, grated
2 tablespoons parsley, chopped
1 tablespoon lemon juice
1/3 cup mayonnaise or salad dressing
6 medium tomatoes
1/4 teaspoon salt
Lettuce

Drain and flake salmon.
Combine all ingredients except tomatoes, salt and lettuce.
Cut centers from tomatoes, salt lightly and fill with the salmon mix-
ture.
Serve in lettuce cups.

Salmon Mousse with Dill Sauce

Dill sauce

Cucumber, peeled, grated , and drained for 1 hour
8 oz (225 g) sour cream
8 oz (225 g) mayonnaise
1 Tbsp fresh lemon juice
1 small clove garlic, minced
1 tsp salt
5 oz (150 g) fresh dill, finely chopped

Salmon mousse

Butter or mayonnaise, for greasing mold
1 envelope unflavored gelatine
50 ml cold water and 100 ml boiling water, for gelatin
4 oz (113 g) mayonnaise
1 Tbsp fresh lemon juice
1 Tbsp fresh lime juice
1 Tbsp grated onion
2 drops tabasco sauce
1/2 tsp smoked paprika
1 tsp salt
1 pound (453 g) flaked smoked salmon
2 Tbsps capers, drained
8 oz (225 g) whipped cream
Lemon slices
Parsley for garnish

1. Dill sauce: combine all the ingredients in a medium bowl. Cover with plastic wrap and chill.
2. Mousse: grease a fish mold with butter or mayonnaise.
3. Soften the gelatin in 50 ml *cold* water. Add 100 ml boiling water and stir well, until the gelatin has dissolved. Add the mayonnaise, lemon juice, lime juice, onion, hot sauce, paprika, and salt and mix well. Add the salmon and capers. Add the whipped cream and continue mixing until everything is well combined. Pour the mixture into the mold. Cover with plastic wrap and chill in the refrigerator for 8 hours or overnight.
4. When ready to serve, un-mold the mousse onto a large plate. Garnish with lemon and parsley.
5. Serve the salmon mousse with the dill sauce.

Smoked Salmon and Cream Cheese

125 g (4.4 oz.) chopped or ground salmon trimmings
125 g (4.4 oz.) cream cheese
125 ml (½ cup) clear consomme
salt, pepper, lemon juice to taste.
Chopped parsley or dill for decoration.

1. Mix warm consomme with cream cheese.
2. Add seasonings, chopped salmon and mix everything together.
3. Place in refrigerator and when set, sprinkle with parsley or dill.

Smoked Salmon with Avocado

125 g (4.4 oz.) finely chopped or ground salmon trimmings
125 g (4.4 oz.) mashed avocado
125 g (4.4 oz.) mayonnaise
Lemon juice, salt, pepper.
Sour cream and croutons for decoration.

Mix all ingredients together and place in refrigerator. When set, garnish with sour cream and arrange croutons around it.

Smoked Salmon Pâté

125 g (4.4 oz.) finely chopped or ground salmon trimmings
75 ml (2 fl oz.) heavy cream
30 ml (1 oz.) single cream
15 ml (1 Tbs.) lemon juice
15 ml (1 Tbs.) vegetable oil
Salt, pepper, pinch of cayenne.

1. In a food processor blend single cream, lemon juice and oil.
2. Add other ingredients and chopped salmon and blend together.
3. Place in containers and refrigerate.

Sheepshead *(Archosargus probatocephalus)*

Name	Protein %	Fat %	Water %
Sheepshead	20.21	2.41	77.97

The sheepshead, also known as convict fish, is a bottom feeding rock fish that reaches 10 to 20 inches with average weight 3 - 4 pounds. It has sharp dorsal spines and 5 to 6 dark bars on the side of the body over a gray background. Sheepshead has several rows of strong teeth, which help crush the shells of oysters, clams, and other bivalves, and barnacles, fiddler crabs, and other crustaceans. Sheepshead like warm waters, they can be found from the Mid-Atlantic to Texas. They are delicious to eat.

Photo 6.41 Sheepshead.

Smoked Sheepshead

Wash the fish and remove the scales. Clean and gut the fish, remove the gills.

Brine for 15 minutes in 80° brine. Wash and drain.

Dry the fish for 60 minutes at 100° F (38° C). A light smoke allowed. Increase the temperature to 212° F (100° C) and smoke with medium dense smoke for 1 hour.

Smoke for additional hour gradually dropping the temperature to 176° F (80° C).

Smoked Sheepshead Fillet

- Fillet the fish.
- Brine the 1/2" fillets for 5 minutes in 80° brine. Wash and drain.
- Dry fillets for 60 minutes in a smokehouse preheated to 100° F (38° C). A light smoke is allowed.
- Smoke for 60 minutes at 185° F (85 C).

Snapper

Name	Protein %	Fat %	Water %
Snapper	20.51	1.34	76.87

The red snapper, *Lutjanus campechanus*, is a prized edible fish found in the Gulf of Mexico and the southeastern Atlantic coast of the United States. The red snapper's body is very similar in shape to other snappers, such as the mangrove snapper, mutton snapper, lane snapper, and dog snapper. The common adult length is 60 cm (23 inch), 9 lb (4 kg).

Photo 6.42 Mangrove snapper.

Smoked Snapper Fillet
- Fillet the fish.
- Brine fillets for 10 minutes in 80° brine. Wash and drain.
- Air dry for 60 minutes.
- Dry fillets for 60 minutes in a smokehouse preheated to 100° F (38° C). A light smoke is allowed.
- Smoke for 90 minutes at 185° F (85° C).

Tilapia

Name	Protein %	Fat %	Water %
Tilapia	20.08	1.70	78.08

Tilapia are mainly freshwater fish, inhabiting shallow streams, ponds, rivers and lakes, and less commonly found living in brackish water. Tilapia are unable to survive in cold climates because they require warm water. In the United States, tilapia are found in much of Florida, Texas and Arizona. Tilapia is an important commercially farm raised fish and is processed into skinless, boneless fillets.

Photo 6.43 Tilapia.

Smoked Tilapia Fillet

- Fillet the fish.
- Brine the 1/2"fillets for 5 minutes in 80° brine. Wash and drain.
- Dry fillets for 60 minutes in a smokehouse preheated to 100° F (38° C). A light smoke is allowed.
- Smoke for 60 minutes at 185° F (85° C).

Tilapia Mousse

2 smoked tilapia fillets
Lemon juice from 2 lemons
Lemon zest (1 lemon)
Gelatin
1/4 pint sour cream
1/4 pint whipped cream
3 egg whites (whisked)
2 Tbsp horseradish
2 Tbsp prepared mustard
2 Tbsp finely diced onions
2 Tbsp chopped capers
1 Tbsp chopped ginger

1. Grease a fish mold with butter or mayonnaise.
2. Soften the gelatin in 50 ml cold water. Add 100 ml boiling water and stir well, until the gelatin has dissolved. Add all ingredients and mix well. Add the whipped cream and continue mixing until everything is well combined. Pour the mixture into the mold. Cover and chill in the refrigerator for 8 hours or overnight.
3. When ready to serve, un-mold the mousse onto a large plate.

Photo 6.44 A nice catch of tilapias taken by casting a net on a golf course lake.

Trout - Rainbow *(Oncorhynchus mykiss)*

Name	Protein %	Fat %	Water %
Trout, rainbow	20.48	3.46	71.87
Trout, rainbow, farmed	19.94	6.18	73.80

Photo 6.45 Farm raised rainbow trout.

There is rainbow, brook and brown trout. Rainbow trout can be found everywhere where there is cold and clean running water, however, it owns its popularity to the fact that it gains weight more quickly than other species of trout, so it is more suitable for fish farming. They reach the market size (25-30 cm) and weight (150-300 g) in less than two years. The average farm raised rainbow trout weighs less than a pound which makes it an ideal fish to be smoked whole. Trout which lives in the wild can reach large size with age.

Brining

The fish is washed, gutted, the head is left on. The brined fish are threaded on speats, through either the eyes or tail, and are hung to allow surplus brine to drain from the fish.

Weight in grams (whole gutted fish)	Time in 80° brine
Small trout 140-200 g	45 minutes
Medium size trout 200-300 g	60 minutes
Large trout, over 300 g	120 minutes

Smoking

The following times apply to factory made smokers with reliable temperature controls. *If smoking in a traditional wood fired smoker, double up the times.*

Smokehouse	Temperature	Time
Drying	86° F (30° C)	30 minutes
Smoking	122° F (50° C)	30 min
Smoking/Cooking	176° F (80° C)	45-60 min

Drying - to allow the skin to dry and to toughen the fish to sufficiently support the weight of the fish during the later stages of smoking. All dampers fully open.

Smoking - inlet and outlet dampers open 1/4 to raise the temperature and humidity so that the fish is not dried too much.

Smoking/Cooking - cooking stage with smoke present. Dampers set as above.

The refrigerated fish will keep in good condition for 1 week.

Dry Salt Curing

Weigh the fish and take 5% salt in relation to the weight. For 1/2 pound (222 g) fish take 12 g (5%) (2 tsp) salt and rub it all around the fish, including the belly.

Cure fish:

1/2 lb (222 g) - 2 hours
3/4 lb (340 g) - 2.5 hours
1 lb (453 g) - 3 hours

Strong brine cures the fish fast, however weaker brines can also be used.

Wet Curing times

4° brine - 10 hours.
20° brine - 2.5 hours.
80° brine - 1 hour.
Use 1 quart of brine per pound of fish.

Rinse the fish, drain and let dry in air for 30 minutes.

- Dry in smokehouse at 100° F (38° C) for 30 minutes.
- Hot smoke at 176° F (80° C) for 1 hour.
- Cook at 176° F (80° C) for 1 hour.

The trout is cooked during hot smoking process which makes it ready for eating without further preparation. Cool in air.

Marinated and Fast Smoked Trout

Make weak (4°) bine, Add dried dill, crushed pepper and crushed juniper berries. Use one teaspoon of spices per one quart of marinade. Marinate for 24 hours.
Rinse the fish briefly and hang to drain and dry for 30 minutes.
Hot smoke at 302° F (150° C) for 30 minutes.

Trout (Adapted from: *Fish Smoking, A Torry Kiln Operator's Handbook,* Her Majesty's Stationery Office).

Small rainbow trout are gutted and the gut cavity cleaned out, care being taken to remove all black skin and blood along the backbone. The fish are brined in an 80° brine for one hour. The brined fish are then pierced through the eyes with metal speats. Small strips of wood like matchsticks are placed between the lug flap to keep the gut cavity open to allow drying and smoke penetration. Trolleys of brined fish are put into the kiln whilst they are still wet with brine. All the fires are lighted and the temperature of the kiln is allowed to rise to about 90° F (32° C). After 30 - 45 minutes when the skins have dried off, the temperature is raised to 180° F (82° C) and the trout are cooked. This takes about two hours. The trout have a lower fat content than herring, and in consequence they should be dried less than buckling or they will tend to be somewhat dry and hard and will lose their soft texture.

Smoked Trout

Gut and clean fish (1 lb. in weight) and place in 80 degrees brine for 2 hours. You may leave fish overnight in 30 degrees brine. Soak for 10 minutes in cold water. Rinse and dry for 2 hours. Start applying smoke and hold at 90° F (32° C) for 15 minutes. Continue smoking increasing temperature until internal temperature of 150° F (66° C) is obtained. Maintain this temperature for 30 minutes. Bigger fish will require longer smoking time.

Note: you can smoke/bake trout at 300–350° F (150–180° C) which will take only 20 minutes, however, little smoky flavor will be obtained.

Trout Cucumber Spread

1 cup flaked smoked fish	1 tsp dry dill
2 cucumbers	2 Tbsp vinegar
1/2 cup sour cream	1 tsp salt
1 Tbsp chopped chives or scallions	1/4 tsp pepper

Peel cucumbers and chop. Blend all ingredients in a food processor.

Photo 6.46 Brad Benter holds wild rainbow trout in Alaska.

U.S. Fish and Wildlife Service.

Tuna

Name	Protein %	Fat %	Water %
Tuna, yellowfin	24	0.49	74.03
Tuna, bluefin	23	4.90	68.09
Tuna, skipjack	22	1.01	70.58

A tuna is a saltwater finfish that belongs to the mackerel family (Scombridae)-which also includes the bonitos, mackerels, and Spanish mackerels. The major types of tuna are: Albacore, Atlantic Bluefin, Skipjack, Yellow Fin and Big Eye. They vary greatly, ranging from the bullet tuna (max. length: 50 cm (1.6 ft), weight: 1.8 kg (4 lb) up to the Atlantic bluefin tuna (max. length: 4.6 m (15 ft), weight: 684 kg (1,508 lb)). Tuna is oo the fastest fish, capable of speeds up to 47 mph (75 km/hr).

Tuna Steak

Brine in 80° brine:

1" thick	-	10 min
1 ½" thick	-	15 min

Rinse and drain. Place on brushed with oil screens.

- Brine the 1"fillets for 10 minutes in 80° brine. Wash and drain.
- Dry fillets for 60 minutes in a smokehouse preheated to 100° F (38° C).
- Smoke for 90 minutes at 180° F (82° C).

Tuna a la King

2 cans (6-1/2 or 7 ounces each) tuna
1/4 cup chopped green pepper
1/4 cup butter or other fat, melted
1/4 cup flour
1 teaspoon salt
Dash pepper
2 cups milk
1/4 cup chopped pimiento
Corn bread, biscuits, or toast

Drain tuna.
Break into large pieces.
Cook green pepper in butter until tender.
Blend in flour, salt and pepper.
Add milk gradually and cook until thick, stirring constantly.
Add pimiento and tuna; heat.
Serve on corn bread, biscuits, or toast.

Tuna a la Stroganoff

2 cans (6-1/2 or 7 ounces each) tuna
1 chicken bouillon cube
1 cup boiling water
1/2 cup chopped onion
1 can (8 ounces) mushroom stems and pieces, drained
1/4 cup butter or other fat, melted
2 tablespoons flour
1/4 teaspoon Worcestershire sauce
2 tablespoons ketchup
Dash pepper
1/2 cup sour cream
2 cups cooked rice

Drain tuna.
Break into large pieces.
Dissolve bouillon cube in boiling water.
Cook onion and mushrooms in butter until tender.
Blend in flour and brown.
Add bouillon gradually and cook until thick, stirring constantly.
Add remaining ingredients, except rice; heat. Serve over rice.

Tuna Canapes Tangy

1 can (6-1/2 or 7 ounces) tuna
1 tablespoon finely chopped celery
3 tablespoon mayonnaise or salad dressing
1/2 cup butter or margarine
3 tablespoons horseradish
32 toast points
Chopped parsley

Drain tuna.
Flake.
Add celery and mayonnaise; blend into a paste.
Combine butter and horseradish.
Spread horseradish butter on toast points.
Top with tuna mixture.
Garnish with parsley sprinkled over the top.

Tuna Canapes with Mushrooms

1 can (6-1/2 or 7 ounces) tuna
1/2 cup condensed mushroom soup
1 tablespoon finely chopped pimiento
1 tablespoon finely chopped green pepper
1/4 teaspoon salt
Dash paprika
32 round crackers
1/2 cup grated cheese

Drain tuna.
Flake.
Add soup, pimiento, green pepper and seasoning; blend into a paste.
Spread on crackers.
Sprinkle with cheese.
Place on a cookie sheet, 15-1/2 x 12 inches.
Broil about 3 inches from source of heat for 5 minutes or until cheese browns.

Tuna Cheese Sandwich

1 can (6-1/2 or 7 ounces) tuna
1/4 cup butter or margarine
1 teaspoon prepared mustard
6 slices bread
1 tablespoon chopped onion
1/2 cup chopped celery
1 tablespoon chopped sweet pickle or sweet pickle relish
1/4 cup mayonnaise or salad dressing
6 slices cheese
Paprika
Parsley sprigs

Drain tuna. Flake.
Cream butter and blend in mustard.
Spread bread with mustard butter.
Combine onion, celery, pickle, mayonnaise and tuna.
Spread bread with tuna mixture and cover with cheese.
Sprinkle with paprika.
Place sandwiches on a cooky sheet, 15-1/2 x 12 inches.
Bake in a very hot oven, 450° F (232° C), for 10 to 12 minutes or
until cheese melts and bread toasts.
Garnish with parsley.

Tuna Dip

1 can (6-1/2 or 7 ounces) tuna
1 tablespoon horseradish
1-1/2 teaspoons onion salt
1 teaspoon Worcestershire sauce
1 cup sour cream
2 teaspoons chopped parsley
Potato chips

Drain tuna.
Flake.
Blend in horseradish, onion salt and Worcestershire sauce.
Fold in sour cream.
Chill.
Garnish with parsley and serve with potato chips.

Tuna Jambalaya

2 cans (6-1/2 or 7 ounces each) tuna
1 cup chopped celery
1/2 cup chopped onion
1/2 cup chopped green pepper
2 cloves garlic, finely chopped
1/4 cup butter or other fat, melted
2 chicken bouillon cubes
1-1/2 cups boiling water
3/4 cup uncooked rice
1 can (1 pound 4 ounces) tomatoes
1/4 teaspoon salt
1 whole bay leaf
1/2 teaspoon crushed thyme
Dash cayenne pepper
1/4 cup chopped parsley

Drain tuna.
Break into large pieces.
Cook celery, onion, green pepper and garlic in butter until tender.
Dissolve bouillon cubes in boiling water.
To the vegetable mixture add rice, tomatoes, salt, bay leaf, thyme,
cayenne pepper and bouillon.
Simmer for 25 to 30 minutes, or until rice is tender. Add parsley and
tuna; heat.

Tuna Molded Salad

2 cans (6-1/2 or 7 ounces each) tuna
2 tablespoons unflavored gelatin
1/2 cup cold water
4 chicken bouillon cubes
1-1/2 cups boiling water
1/2 cup mayonnaise or salad dressing
3 hard boiled eggs, chopped
1/2 cup sliced stuffed olives
3/4 cup chopped celery
3/4 cup cooked peas
Salad greens
Sliced stuffed olives
Tomato wedges

Drain tuna.

Break into large pieces.

Soften gelatin in cold water for 5 minutes.

Dissolve bouillon cubes in boiling water; add gelatin and stir until dissolved.

Chill until almost congealed.

Add mayonnaise, eggs, olives, celery, peas and tuna.

Place in a 1-1/2 quart mold; chill until firm.

Unmold on salad greens; garnish with olives and tomatoes.

Tuna Mousse

20 ml gelatine
100 ml water
60 g tomato soup mix
125 ml cottage cheese

250 ml mayonnaise
1 small green peppers
1 onions
3 celery rib
2 egg
340 g light chunk tuna in water
0.50 teaspoon Tabasco sauce
50 ml coffee creamer

Combine gelatine and 100 ml water in a bowl placed over a container of boiling water and mix until dissolved.

In a separate pan bring the soup to a boil and stir until thickened.

Add gelatine to soup and allow to cool.

Add all other ingredients and pour into an oiled (preferably fish-shaped) mold.

Allow to set completely in the fridge.

Turn out on a platter and garnish with prawns and lemon slices.

Serve with crusty bread or melba toast.

Tuna Pineapple Dip

1 can (6-1/2 or 7 ounces) tuna
1 can (9 ounces) crushed pineapple
1 package (8 ounces) cream cheese
3 tablespoons pineapple juice
Dash salt
Dash nutmeg
Potato chips

Drain tuna.
Flake.
Drain pineapple and save liquid.
Soften cheese at room temperature.
Combine all ingredients except potato chips; blend into a paste.
Chill.
Serve in a bowl surrounded by potato chips.

Tuna Salad

2 cans (6-1/2 or 7 ounces each) tuna
1/2 cup mayonnaise or salad dressing
1 cup chopped celery
2 tablespoons chopped sweet pickle
2 tablespoons chopped onion
2 hard boiled eggs, chopped
1/2 teaspoon salt
Dash pepper
Lettuce
1 hard boiled egg, sliced

Drain tuna.
Break into large pieces.
Combine all ingredients except lettuce and egg.
Serve on lettuce; garnish with egg slices.

Tuna Slaw

2 cans (6-1/2 or 7 ounces each) tuna
2 cups shredded cabbage
1/4 cup chopped green pepper
2 tablespoons grated onion
1/2 teaspoon salt
Dash pepper
1/2 cup mayonnaise or salad dressing

Drain tuna.
Break into large pieces.
Combine all ingredients.

Tuna Souffle Salad

2 cans (6-1/2 or 7 ounces each) tuna
1 package lemon flavored gelatin
1 cup boiling water
1/2 cup cold water
2 tablespoons vinegar
1/4 teaspoon salt
Dash pepper
1/2 cup mayonnaise or salad dressing
1 tablespoon grated onion
1/2 cup chopped celery
1/4 cup chopped parsley
Salad greens
Mayonnaise or French dressing

Drain tuna.
Break into large pieces.
Dissolve gelatin in boiling water.
Add cold water, vinegar, salt, pepper and mayonnaise.
Blend well with rotary beater.
Chill until almost congealed.
Whip with rotary beater until fluffy.
Fold in onion, celery, parsley and tuna.
Place in a 1-quart ring mold; chill until firm.
Unmold on salad greens.
Serve with mayonnaise or French dressing

Tuna Tossed Salad

2 cans (6-1/2 or 7 ounces each) tuna
1 clove garlic
1 cup drained bean sprouts
1/2 cup chopped cucumber
1 cup celery crescents
2 cups chopped raw spinach
1/4 cup chopped green onion
1/2 cup French dressing
Tomato wedges

Drain tuna.
Break into large pieces.
Rub the inside of a salad bowl with the cut surface of a clove of garlic.
Combine all ingredients except tomatoes.
Garnish with tomato wedges.

Tuna with Noodles

2 cans (6-1/2 or 7 ounces each) tuna
1 package (8 ounces) noodles
2 tablespoons butter or other fat
2 tablespoons flour
1/2 teaspoon salt
Dash pepper
1-1/2 cups milk
2 teaspoons grated orange rind
1/2 teaspoon grated lemon rind
2 tablespoons orange juice
Orange segments
Parsley sprigs

Drain tuna.
Break into large pieces.
Cook noodles as directed on package; drain.
Melt butter; blend in flour and seasonings.
Add milk gradually and cook until thick and smooth, stirring constantly.
Add orange and lemon rind, orange juice, noodles, and tuna; heat.
Garnish with orange segments and parsley sprigs.

Tuna with Rice

2 cans (6-1/2 or 7 ounces each) tuna
2 tablespoons chopped onion
2 tablespoons butter or other fat, melted
2 tablespoons flour
1-1/2 cups milk
3/4 cup grated cheese
3 cups cooked rice
Cheese sauce
Paprika
Chopped parsley

Drain tuna.
Break into large pieces.
Cook onion in butter until tender.
Blend in flour.
Add milk gradually and cook until thick, stirring constantly.
Add cheese and heat until cheese melts.
Stir in tuna; heat.
Serve over rice.
Top with cheese sauce.
Garnish with paprika and parsley sprinkled over the top.

Tuna Waldorf Salad

2 cans (6-1/2 or 7 ounces each) tuna
1 cup diced apples
1/2 cup chopped celery
1/4 cup chopped nutmeats*
1/2 cup mayonnaise or salad dressing
Lettuce

Drain tuna.
Break into large pieces.
Combine all ingredients except lettuce.
Serve on lettuce.

* nutmeat is the edible kernel of a nut, for example peanut.

Whiting *(Merlangius merlangus)*

Name	Protein %	Fat %	Water %
Whiting	18.3	1.31	80.27

Whiting is a cod family fish that is native to the northeastern Atlantic Ocean. Whiting is very similar to Alaska Pollock *(Theragra chalcogramma)*. This fish can reach a maximum length of about 70 cm (28 inches). Whiting and Alaska Pollock are commonly used in the fast food industry, for example the Filet-O-Fish sandwich and Fish McBites at McDonald's.

Smoked Whiting Fillet

- Fillet the fish.
- Brine the 1/2" fillets for 5 minutes in 80° brine. Wash and drain.
- Dry fillets for 60 minutes in a smokehouse preheated to 100° F (38° C). A light smoke is allowed.
- Smoke for 60 minutes at 180° F (82° C).

Whiting Salad

1 pound smoked whiting flakes
1/2 cup mayonnaise
2 hard boiled eggs, chopped
1 cup chopped celery
1 Tbsp creamy horseradish
2 tablespoons chopped sweet pickle
2 tablespoons chopped onion
1/2 teaspoon salt
Dash pepper

Garnish:
Lettuce
1 hard boiled egg, sliced

Combine all ingredients except lettuce and one egg.
Serve on lettuce; garnish with egg slices.

SHELLFISH - Clams

Name	Protein %	Fat %	Water %
Clam	14.67	0.96	78.98

There is a great variety of clams that find the way to to the dinner table. Some, like beautiful Coquina *(Donax)* clams in West Florida are very small and are suitable for clam chowder soup only, others like Sand Clam *(Spisula solidissima raveneli)*, Sunray Clam *(Macrocallista nimbosa)* or Quahog Clam *(Mercenaria campachiensis)* can be cooked or smoked.

Photo 6.47 Littleneck clams.

The clams are abundant in most areas of the world. The Pacific razor clam *(Siliqua patula)* is an exceptionally meaty shellfish which ranges from California to Alaska.

Cleaning Clams

Make 10° brine - 1/3 cup of non-iodized salt (iodine will kill clams) to one gallon (3.8 liters) of water. Soak clams in the brine for 20 minutes. Pour the clams into a strainer, and rinse with cold water. Scrub thoroughly with a stiff brush. Place clams on the towel and rub them dry to remove any final grit.

Photo 6.48 Place cleaned clams into a double pot steamer or a large kettle. Add half a cup of water for every pound (453 g) of clams. Cover the kettle and apply high heat. Steam the clams until they open their shells.

Depending on the type of clams, this may take from 3 to 10 minutes. Remove the open clams and serve. Discard any unopened clams as they probably were already dead.

Shucking. Many people enjoy eating raw clams and oysters. If you are shucking your own, the shells will be easier to open if you freeze them for 10 to 15 minutes or place them in refrigerator for 20-30 minutes.

Remove them from freezer and let sit a few minutes before further processing. As they warm up, the muscles relax and the shells will open slightly so you can get your clam knife in. You have to, however, be fast as the moment you pick them up they will start closing up.

Photo 6.49 Warmed up mussel.

For the time being you may just insert a popsicle in to prevent the shells from closing.

Photo 6.50 Wooden skewer prevents the shell from closing.

Insert the knife on either side and using the point cut as close to the shell as possible. This will detach the muscle from the shell. Now, the shell can be open with the fingers. Perform this operation over a bowl to save all that wonderful juice known as clam liquor.

Smoking Clams

- Clean the clams
- Steam the clams until they open.
- Brine for 3-5 minutes in 40° brine.
- Drain and pat dry. Dip in oil. Drain.
- Preheat smokehouse to 100° F (38° C) and dry the clams without smoke for 30 minutes.
- Increase temperature to 180° F (82° C) and apply a heavy smoke for 30 minutes.

Smoked Clams with Oil and Garlic

Smoked clams
Clam half-shells
Chopped garlic
Parsley

Place half-shells filled with
smoked clams around the plate.
Heat up the olive oil and add
garlic. Pour oil over the clams
and sprinkle parsley over.

Photo 6.51 Smoked clams with
olive oil, garlic and parsley.

Smoked Clams with Curry Butter

Smoked clams
Clam half-shells
Curry butter

Place half-shells filled with smoked clams around the plate.
Melt the curry, garlic or parsley butter.
Pour the hot butter over the clams.

Photo 6.52 Assortment of smoked clams and mussels with garlic,
parsley and curry butters.

Mussels *(Mytilus edulis)*

Name	Protein %	Fat %	Water %
Mussels	11.90	2.24	80.58

The shell of the mussel is elongated and asymmetrical compared with clams, which are often more or less rounded or oval. The most popular is the Blue Mussel *(Mytilus edulis)*, also known as the common mussel. The shell is smooth, and blue-black in color; young mussels are sometimes yellowish-brown with blue-black bands. The mussel reaches marketable size after about three years' growth, when it is two inches or more in length.

Photo 6.53 Blue mussels.

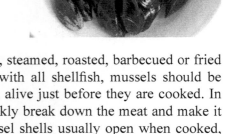

Mussels can be smoked, boiled, steamed, roasted, barbecued or fried in butter or vegetable oil. As with all shellfish, mussels should be checked to ensure they are still alive just before they are cooked. In dead mussels the enzymes quickly break down the meat and make it unpalatable or poisonous. Mussel shells usually open when cooked, revealing the cooked soft parts. Live mussels, when in the air, will shut tightly when disturbed. Open, unresponsive mussels are dead, and must be discarded.

Most mussels are farmed and are less likely to have sand and grit in them, compared to wild mussels. If you gather your own or buy wild mussels, you need to get the grit out - they need to be soaked in a bowl of cold water for about 20 minutes, and then drained. For both types, scrub the mussels under cold, running water and remove the beards (the bristly material sticking out from one side) by pulling down toward the hinge of the shell and outward. If the mussel shell is slightly open, tap it with a knife to see if it closes. If it does not close, discard it - the mussel is dead.

Cooking Mussels

Wash and steam mussels in a little water in a covered kettle for about 5 minutes. Cool the mussels quickly by water spray to prevent toughening of the meat.

The classic method for cooking mussels is steaming them. Mussels contain a small amount of liquid/moisture, so steaming doesn't require the addition of any extra liquid. But typically a small amount of liquid (water, stock, wine, beer) can be added to a hot pan before adding your mussels. Cover tightly with a lid and steam for 5 minutes. The mussels should open between 5 and 7 minutes. Once open, they're cooked and ready to eat. Mussels that don't open should be discarded - they're dead. The meats are removed from the now open shells, usually by hand, and the beard or byssus pulled out. Wash the meats in clean fresh water, but do not leave them soaking in water or they will lose flavour and appear less attractive.

Smoking Mussels

- Steam the mussels until they open.
- Brine for 3-5 minutes in 50° brine.
- Drain and pat dry. Brush or dip shrimp in oil and spread on wire screens. Preheat smokehouse to 100° F (38° C) and dry the mussels without smoke for 25 minutes.
- Increase temperature to 180° F (82° C) and apply a heavy smoke for 30 minutes.

Smoked Mussels with Garlic Butter

Smoked mussels
Clam half-shells
Lemon
Parsley

Place half-shells filled with smoked mussels around the plate. Garnish with lemon wedges and parsley. Melt down the garlic butter and pour it over the mussels.

Photo 6.54 Smoked mussels with garlic and olive oil.

Oysters

Name	Protein %	Fat %	Water %
Oyster, eastern	5.71	1.71	89.04
Oyster, eastern, farmed	5.22	1.55	86.20
Oyster, Pacific	9.45	2.30	82.06

Oyster are distributed world wide and can weigh from 35 to 100 g.

English - grow in cold water *(Ostrea edulis)*
Portuguese - grow in warm water *(Crassostrea angulata)*
Pacific - grow in warm water *(Crassostrea gigas)*
Olympia oysters (Pacific) - *(Ostrea conchaphila)*

Photo 6.55 Oysters look like pieces of marine rock covered with barnacles.

Photo 6.56 Oyster knife has a strong blade and a finfer protection ring.

Oysters can survive out of water for weeks if carefully handled and kept moist and cool. They should be carried and stored with the cupped half of the shell downwards, and kept moist by covering with a damp cloth. Oysters should be refrigerated out of water, not frozen, and in 100% humidity. Oysters stored in water under refrigeration will open, consume available oxygen, and die. Oysters must be eaten alive, or cooked alive. Oysters can be eaten on the half shell, raw, smoked, boiled, baked, fried, roasted, stewed, canned, pickled, steamed, or broiled, or used in a variety of drinks. Eating can be as simple as opening the shell and eating the contents, including juice.

The shells of live oysters are normally tightly closed or snap shut given a slight tap. Open oysters should be tapped on the shell; a live oyster will close up and is safe to eat. Oysters which are open and unresponsive are dead and must be discarded. Cooking oysters in the shell kills the oysters and causes them to open by themselves.

Shucking *(Opening)*

Oyster lovers insist that the only way to enjoy them is raw, with lemon juice, vinegar, or cocktail sauce. This, of course, eliminates cooking them. Refrigerate oysters for 1 hour to help them relax. Relaxing the muscles to shuck oysters is faster if you place them in a freezer for about 15 minutes.

Photo 6.57 At first look opening an oyster may look difficult, but it is quite easy due to a little gap between the halves in the back by the hinge (see the white arrow).

Photo 6.58 Take a pointed oyster knife in one hand and thick towel or glove in the other. With towel, grip shell in palm of hand. Keeping oyster level with knife, insert the tip of a short bladed oyster knife between shell halves next to the hinge.

Photo 6.59 Twist the knife to break the hinge and to pry the shell apart.

The knife is then used to sever the adductor muscle at its point of attachment to first the flat half of the shell, then the cupped half. Discard the top shell. Cut the muscle from the lower shell, being careful not to spill oyster liquor if the oyster is to be eaten raw.

Photo 6.60 Cut the muscle from the lower shell, being careful not to spill oyster liquor if the oyster is to be eaten raw.

If live oysters are to be used in a cooked dish, rather than for eating raw, you can steam them just until the shells open. Then cut them from the shells and proceed.

Smoked Oysters

Handling oyster muscle is difficult as the oysters contain around 90% water. They are soft and slippery and easily tear apart. For these reasons it is advantageous to firm them up by brief cooking:

- Steam oyster shells for 20 minutes, then remove the oyster muscles.
- Brine oysters for 3-5 minutes in 40° brine.
- Drain and pat dry.
- Dip in oil. Drain. Place on wire mesh screen.
- Preheat smokehouse to 100-120° F (38-49° C) and dry the oysters without smoke for 60 minutes.
- Increase temperature to 180° F (82° C) and apply a heavy smoke for 30 minutes.

Smoked Oysters (Adapted from: *Fish Smoking, A Torry Kiln Operator's Handbook,* Her Majesty's Stationery Office).

A considerable proportion of the total production of oysters in Britain consists of misshapen native oysters or of Portuguese oysters that do not command the high price of quality natives. In America these second grade shellfish are frequently smoked and packed in oil to make a popular delicatessen product.

The oysters should first be cleansed to ensure that there is no risk of food poisoning from them, are steamed in a cooker for 20 to 30 minutes. The meats are then picked and brined in a 50° brine for 5 minutes.

They are quickly dipped in oil and spread on wire mesh trays. They are smoked for 30 minutes in a dense smoke at 180° F (82 C), the kiln being raised to this temperature before smoking begins. During the smoking, the oysters should be turned over, to ensure uniform smoking. The smoked meats are packed in small jars, covered with good quality edible oil, and the jars sterilized at 15 lb pressure for 15 minutes.

Smoked Oysters on Potato Chips

8 oz (225 g) smoked oysters
Pringles® Sour Cream Potato Chips
Sour cream
1 Tbsp chopped chives

Lay chips on a serving plate. Top each with an oyster. sour cream and a sprinkle of chives.

Photo 6.61 Smoked oysters with sour cream on potato chips.

Smoked Oysters with Lemon Butter

Photo 6.62 Oysters with clarified lemon butter.

Note: Herbs that go well with oysters include thyme, fennel seed, paprika, and parsley.

Scallops

Name	Protein %	Fat %	Water %
Scallops	12.06	0.49	82.53

Scallops are characterized by having two types of meat in one shell: the adductor muscle, called "scallop", which is white and meaty, and the roe, called "coral", which is red or white and soft. Outside the U.S., the scallop is often sold whole. In the UK and Australia, they are available both with and without the roe. The roe is also usually eaten. The energy corporation Royal Dutch Shell scallop shell logo is displayed on every gasoline station.

The largest wild scallop fishery is for the Atlantic sea scallop (*Placopecten magellanicus*) found off northeastern United States and eastern Canada. Most of the rest of the world's production of scallops is from Japan (wild, enhanced, and aquaculture), and China (mostly cultured Atlantic bay scallops).

Scallops are always sold pre-shucked from the shell. They cannot be kept live, because they must scoot around in the water to live.

Photo 6.63 Small and large scallops.

Processing your own catch:

- Turn the scallop so that the darker side of the shelled scallop is facing upwards.
- Take a knife or sharpened spoon and insert it between the top and bottom halves of the shell.
- Force the shell open. Cut away the scallop's muscle in the top half of the shell and throw the top half of the shell away.
- Clean the inside of the scallop shell of everything but the white muscle.
- Detach the muscle from the shell.
- Rinse the scallop under cold water.

Use herbs, spices, and sauces sparingly so as not to overpower the delicate flavor of the scallops. If you are using them in a chowder, add them last and cook only until they turn white. Large sea scallops will take 3 to 5 minutes in a hot skillet to saute, while the smaller bay scallops will take only 1 to 2 minutes. Overcooking scallops makes them tough and rubbery.

Smoked Scallops

- Brine scallops for 3-5 minutes in 40° brine.
- Drain and pat dry. Dip in oil. Drain.
- Preheat smokehouse to 120° F (49° C) and dry the scallops without smoke for 30 minutes.
- Increase temperature to 180° F (82° C) and apply a heavy smoke for 30 - 45 minutes.

Scallops with Butter Sauces

Melt down the parsley or garlic butter and pour it over the scallops.

Scallops with Citrus Sauce

Fill the empty orange shell with scallops. Pour hot citrus sauce over the smoked scallops.

Photo 6.64 Small and large scallops with cocktail sauce.

Shrimp

Shrimp are swimming crustaceans with long narrow muscular abdomens and long antennae. Unlike crabs and lobsters, shrimp are more adapted for swimming than walking. They look somewhat like small lobsters, but not like crabs. There are thousands of species, but only a few types are sold commercially. More shrimp are farmed today than harvested in the wild.

The most widely cultured species in the world are:

- Giant shrimp, *Penaeus monodon,* typically 25–30 cm (10–12 in) long, 200–320 g (7–11 oz).

- Whiteleg shrimp, Litopenaeus vannamei, 23 cm (9.1 in).

Photo 6.65 Small pink shrimp on the left, larger white shrimp on the right.

Smoking the delicate shrimp presents a problem as they are cooked within minutes. Put shrimp in boiling water 212° F (100° C) and they'll be done in about 3 minutes. If they are overcooked, they'll have a rubbery texture.

Heat transfer in air is much slower than in water so the cooking time in a smokehouse must be extended. Smoking shrimp for 10 minutes in preheated to 212° F (100° C) smokehouse will cook them.

Note: if your smokehouse can maintain the temperature of 180° F (82° C) use the hot smoking method, otherwise boil the shrimp and cold smoke.

Hot Smoked Shrimp

- Peel shrimp.
- Brine shrimp for 3 minutes in 50° brine.
- Drain and pat dry.
- Dip in oil. Drain. Place on a wire screen.
- Preheat smokehouse to 100° F (38° C) and dry the shrimp without smoke for 30 minutes.
- Increase temperature to 180° F (82° C) and apply a heavy smoke for 30 minutes.

Cold Smoked Shrimp

- Peel shrimp
- Boil for 3 minutes, depending on a size, in a 40° brine (10 percent salt solution)
- Drain and dry for 1 hour.
- Brush or dip shrimp in oil and spread on wire screens.
- Smoke for 60 minutes at 85° F (30° C).

Smoked Shrimp With Cocktail Sauce

Photo 6.66 Smoked shrimp with cocktail sauce.

Squid (*Loligo opalescens*)

Name	Protein %	Fat %	Water %
Scallops	15.58	1.38	78.55

Biologically, squid belong to the class of mollusks known as cephalopods, which also include octopus. Squid found along Washington's coast, the Strait of Juan de Fuca and Puget Sound are called Pacific squid, opalescent, or-most commonly-market squid. Adult market squid found in inside waters average about eight inches (mantle plus tentacles).

The Humboldt species of squid is usually found off the coasts of central and South America but has extended its range to the north, mainly during the late summer and early fall months when the water temperatures are at their highest.

Photo 6.67 Squid.

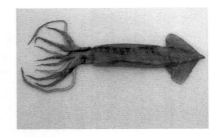

Smoked Squid *(Adapted from Tanikawa, 1985, Marine Products in Japan).*

Remove head, viscera and tendons from body. Cut off fins. Wash with freshwater. Soak fish for 10-20 min in hot water 122-131° F (50-55° C), with agitation, to remove skin. Wash and boil at 176-194° F (80-90° C) for 2-3 minutes. For 3.75 kg (8.25 lb) boiled squid, mix 200-250 g salt, 750-940 g sugar. 37 g sodium glutamate, and 3.7 g sodium 5-ribonucleotide. Season by sprinkling with seasoning materials, pile in 2-3 layers on a table, and apply light pressure on the squid. Hang the squid in smokehouse and smoke at 68-77° F (20-25° C) for the first 1-2 hours, at 122-140° F (50-60° C) for 4 hours, and at 140-158° F (60-70° C) for the final 2-3 hours. Cut smoked squid into rings, 1-2 mm wide. Mix 357 g sugar, 100-110 g salt, 3.7 g sodium glutamate, 0.4 g sodium 5-ribonucleotide, and 500 ml water and sprinkle on smoked squid. Dry the surfaces in a dryer.

Lobster Tails

Photo 6.68 Lobster tails.

Note: if your smokehouse can maintain the temperature of 180° F (82° C) use the hot smoking method, otherwise boil the lobster tails and apply cold/warm smoke.

Hot Smoking

Using scissors cut the shell open and remove meat.
Brine for 5 minutes in a 40° brine (10 per cent salt solution). Drain.
Dry for 30 minutes in a preheated to 120° F (49° C) smokehouse (no smoke applied).
Increase temperature to 180° F (82° C) and apply a heavy smoke for 30 minutes.

Cold/Warm Smoking

Boil lobster tail in 5° brine (1 Tbsp salt per quart of water) until they turn red. Depending on a size it may take from 5-8 minutes).
Using scissors cut the shell open and remove meat.
Cool in cold water. Drain.
Dry for 30 minutes in a smokehouse preheated to about 120° F (49° C) - no smoke applied.
Smoke with cold/warm smoke for 30 minutes.

Photo 6.69 Smoked lobster tail with clarified lemon butter.

Fish Roe

When cleaning your own catch you will often find roe and milt inside. Whether it is large Pacific salmon roe, smaller Delaware river shad or Florida mullet or perch roe, they all are delicious food that can be prepared in many ways. The milt, or buckroe (the part of the male fish which corresponds to the egg mass of the female) is as common as the female roe or eggs. It compares very favorably in food value with the roe and flesh of the fish. The use of roe or spawn of fish, preserved by salting or pickling, is many centuries old. The name caviare is of Tartar origin and the preparation of sturgeon roe is a huge industry in Russia. Mullet roe and milt are exported in large numbers every winter from Florida to Japan.

Cod Roes (Adapted from: *Fish Smoking, A Torry Kiln Operator's Handbook,* Her Majesty's Stationery Office).

Cod roes must be handled very carefully before salting to avoid bursting their delicate skins.The roes are washed in cold water and are then covered with dry salt. They are usually salted in layers in boxes up to about two feet deep and are left for about six to eight hours. After salting, the roes are placed in large-mesh baskets and thoroughly washed in cold water. The baskets of washed roes are then dipped for a minute or two into very hot or even boiling water. This makes the roes swell and gives them a plump appearance. Dye is sometimes added to the hot water in order to produce a more uniform color. They are then either hung over speats of wood or laid on wire mesh trays and smoked at 90-100° F (32-38° C) for six to eight hours with all the fires alight.

Large Roe, Cooked

Take one or two pair of large roe, of which the skin is unbroken, and dip each piece into heavily salted milk, then into finely sifted bread crumbs. Place in an oiled baking pan, sprinkle liberally with oil and bake in a very hot oven ten to fifteen minutes, according to the thickness of the roe.

Large Roe, with Bacon

Proceed the same as above, except to sprinkle the uncooked roe over with sliced bacon cut in small pieces, instead of the oil. Remove to platter, garnish with sprigs of parsley and pieces of lemon and serve with tartar sauce.

Salad of Fish Roe

If any of the larger roe is left, dice it, mix with twice the amount of finely minced celery and mayonnaise. Season with salt and plenty of lemon juice. Dust on top with paprika.

Small Pieces of Roe

Small roe, two to three inches long by one in width, have been pronounced as delicately flavored as the finest fried oysters. Several at a time may be dipped into the salted milk, dripped a moment, and then into finely sifted bread crumbs, arranged side by side in an oiled baking pan, sprinkled over with oil and baked in a hot oven about eight minutes. Arrange in center of platter with a border of parsley or celery leaves for a garnish and serve with tartar sauce.

Creamed Roe on Toast

Parboil in salted, acidulated water ten minutes, drain, and when cold cut into pieces. Make a white sauce by heating two tablespoons of oil, mixing with it two tablespoons of flour to each cup of milk. Season with salt, pepper, lemon juice, Worcestershire sauce, mushroom, tomato ketchup or any preferred seasoning. Add the pieces of roe, and when heated through serve on piece of toast.

Scalloped Roe and Oysters

1 cup parboiled roe, picked free from skin	1 cup milk (may be canned milk, diluted)
1 cup oysters	1 teaspoon tomato ketchup
2 tablespoons oil or butter	Salt and pepper
3 tablespoons flour	Lemon juice

Heat the oil, add the flour, stir into a roux, add the hot milk. Heat the cup of oysters until edges curl, strain off the oyster liquor, add it to the white sauce, add the oysters, the pieces of roe and the seasonings. Blend well together. Put in individual ramekins or baking dish. Sprinkle over with bread crumbs which have been mixed with a little oil and salt, or a potato border may be piped with a pastry bag around the edge, with crumbs in the center. Bake ten minutes until crumbs are browned.

Mullet Roe

Italians prepare the roe of mullet as a table delicacy, calling it "botargo," derived from the Arabic word "butarih." Mullet roe sometimes called the poor man's caviar is a desired item in many countries: Greece (avgotaracho), Korea (myeongran), East Asia (karasumi), Spain (botarga), French (boutarque) and many more. Mullet roe is yellow in color, very delicate and rather large compared to roe found in other fish. When cleaning the fish, save every particle of the roe, it may be parboiled in salted, slightly acidulated water (with vinegar or lemon juice) and then boiled around 8 minutes. Drain, and when cold pick out the pieces of membrane. Add a tablespoon of mayonnaise and mix to a paste. This will taste great on toast or in any kind of sandwich.

Mullet Milt

Take a pair of mullet milt, cut in two, lengthwise. Our objective in cutting is to prevent them from curling up when cooking. Then dip each piece into salted milk, then into fine bread crumbs, place on an oiled baking pan, sprinkle over with oil and bake in a very hot oven ten to twelve minutes, according to thickness. Garnish with parsley and pieces of lemon. Serve with tartar sauce.

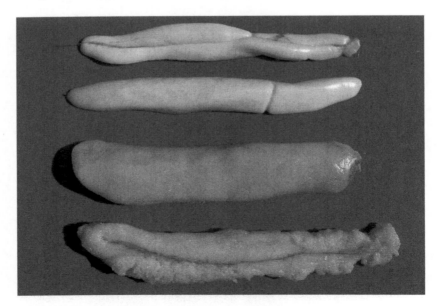

Photo 6.70 Mullet milt top, mullet roe bottom.

Creamed Milt on Toast or in Ramekin

Parboil in salted and acidulated (with lemon juice or vinegar) water for ten minutes. When cold take out skin and cut into cubes. Make a white sauce with two tablespoons of oil or butter and two tablespoons of flour to each cup of milk. Mix the white sauce and cut-up milt together and season with salt, pepper, lemon juice, Worcestershire Sauce and some tomato ketchup. Serve on pieces of toast which have been first dipped into boiling water, then buttered. Or it may be served in individual ramekins with a top dressing of oiled or buttered crumbs and browned in an oven for ten minutes.

Flounder or Sole Roe, Creamed with Green Peas

1 cup roe, cut in pieces, parboiled and free from skin
1 cup green peas
3 tablespoons oil or butter
3 tablespoons flour
1 cup milk

1/3 cup cream
1/2 teaspoon Worcestershire
Sauce
1 teaspoon lemon juice
1 teaspoon tomato ketchup
Salt and pepper

Heat the milk and cream. Melt the butter, sift in the flour, add the hot milk and cream, stirring well until very smooth. Add the pieces of roe, add the cup of green peas, season to taste and serve on pieces of toast, or in individual ramekins.

Creamed Roe, with Shrimps

1 cup parboiled roe, free from
skin and cut in pieces
1 cup shrimp meat, fresh or
canned, cut in pieces
4 tablespoons flour

4 tablespoons oil or butter
2 cups milk
2 teaspoons anchovy essence
1 teaspoon lemon juice
Salt and pepper

Put the milk on to heat. In another saucepan heat the oil or butter. Sift in the flour, stir together, add the hot milk, whipping together until very smooth. Add the roe and the shrimps, season with the anchovy essence, which will color it slightly pink, and the lemon juice, salt and pepper. Serve on toast.

SAUCES

The technique of making *roux* is the first step towards making sauces, gravies or thickening soups.

Drawn Butter or Roux

3 Tbsp. butter (or oil)
2 Tbsp. flour
1 cup boiling water
Salt and pepper to taste

1. Melt *two* tablespoons butter, stir in the flour and allow to bubble up and cook together. *This roux is now ready for the addition of liquid,* which may be water, milk, fish stock, chicken stock, wine, etc.

2. Add the boiling water (or other liquid) and beat until smooth. Add the remaining *tablespoon* of butter, whisking until it is all worked in. Season with salt and pepper. This is a delightful sauce to serve with boiled fish, asparagus, or cauliflower *and can be used for making other sauces.*

In the following examples you can see how simple making a sauce can be:

Caper Sauce

Make *Drawn Butter* sauce and add a tablespoonful of capers to it. Goes well with fish or boiled mutton.

Egg Sauce

Make *Drawn Butter* sauce and add two hard-boiled eggs, chopped fine. Great for fish or poultry.

Hollandaise Sauce

Make Drawn Butter sauce and stir in additional butter, egg yolks and lemon juice to make a thick, yellow, custard like sauce with slight acidity.

Mustard Sauce

Make Drawn Butter and add mustard.

Parsley Sauce

Make Drawn Butter and add finely minced parsley.

Well Known Sauces

Aioli Sauce

2 cloves garlic
1 pinch salt
2 egg yolks
1 tablespoon lemon juice
1 cup oil (olive, vegetable or mixed)

1. Peel the garlic, put in a mortar and pestle with the salt and grind it into a paste.
2. In a mixing bowl whisk the egg yolks, lemon juice, and garlic mixture together until well combined.
3. Start adding the olive oil, drop by drop, whisking all the time. You can add it a bit faster as you go along, but the key to success is going slowly at the beginning.

Note: you can easily see that making Aioli is basically the same as making mayonnaise. So it should come as no surprise that the fastest way to make Aioli Sauce is to mix garlic paste with prepared mayonnaise. Aioli is a very popular sauce in France, Italy and in Spain.

Anchovy Sauce

Make *Drawn Butter* and add a 2 oz can of anchovies.

A fish sauce will have a better flavor if the *fish stock* is added to the *roux*. Make note that you would not add fish stock to let's say Hollandaise Sauce when serving it with chicken and broccoli, but it is fine to add fish stock when making Hollandaise Fish Sauce.

To make fish stock for sauces:

White fish trimmings, backbones of filleted fish, heads (gills removed), fins and tail pieces.

1 onion
1 celery
1 carrot
1 bay leaf
1 sprig of parsley
1 sprig of thyme

1. Place all ingredients in a pot and cover with cold water.
2. Bring to a boil, then simmer for one hour.

3. Filter through a fine strainer or a cheese cloth.

Note: fish stock freezes well.

Anchovy Sauce

3 Tbsp butter or oil
4 Tbsp flour
2 cups milk, or milk and fish stock, equal parts
One 2 oz. can anchovies
Salt and pepper to taste

1. Heat the oil or butter, stir in the flour, stir and allow to cook together.
2. Add all liquid all at once and whisk well with cook's whip until smooth.
3. Add anchovies and seasonings, mix until smooth.

Easy Anchovy Sauce

5 Tbsp anchovy paste or 4 anchovy fillets
1 cup mayonnaise or sour cream

Mix the anchovy paste with mayonnaise until smooth

Bechamel Sauce

This is a classic creamy white sauce which goes well with fish and vegetables.

1 onion
1 carrot
1 celery stick
½ tsp. black pepper corns
⅓ tsp. nutmeg or mace
1½ cup of milk
2 Tbsp. butter
⅓ cup flower
3 Tbsp cream
1 bay leaf
1 strip of lemon zest
Salt and pepper to taste

1. Chop onion, celery and carrot very finely. Add nutmeg, bay leaf, peppercorns, lemon zest and place all in a saucepan. Add milk and bring to a boil. Remove from stove, cover and let sit for 30 minutes.
2. Melt the butter in a saucepan, remove from heat and stir in the flour. Heat again and cook until the mixture thickens (1-2 minutes). This is known as making "roux."
3. Strain milk and vegetables through a fine strainer into a bowl.
4. Blend the milk gradually into the roux, stirring constantly. Bring to a boil and stir until the mixture thickens. Simmer gently additional 3 minutes.
5. Remove the source pan from heat. Season with salt and pepper and stir in the cream.

Note: when serving with fish half of the milk may be replaced with fish stock.

Caper Sauce

2 cups milk, or milk and fish stock, equal parts
3 Tbsp oil
4 Tbsp flour
½ cup capers
1 tsp lemon juice
Salt and pepper

1. Warm up the milk (don't boil).
2. Heat the oil, stir in the flour and cook together, making roux.
3. Add the hot liquid, whisking until smooth.
4. Season with salt and pepper, adding capers and lemon juice.

Celery Cream Sauce

1 cup milk
½ cup cream
½ cup reduced celery water (saved after boiling celery)
1 Tbsp minced parsley
1 cup celery pulp (which has been boiled and rubbed through a sieve)
3 Tbsp oil
4 Tbsp flour
1 Tbsp butter
Salt and pepper

1. Heat the milk and celery water.
2. Heat the oil, stir in the flour and cook together, adding hot liquid and whisking until smooth.
3. Add the celery pulp, the cream, and the butter in small bits, stirring until all blended together.
4. Season with salt and pepper, adding the parsley just before serving.

Citrus Sauce

Zest from 1/2 orange
Juice from 1/2 orange
1 tsp lemon juice
1 clove garlic, finely minced
1/2 tsp chopped ginger
1 teaspoons chopped fresh parsley or tarragon
1 stick butter
Freshly ground black pepper to taste
Salt to taste

Melt the butter in a small saucepan over medium-low heat. Add all ingredients and simmer for 5 minutes.

Cocktail Sauce

1/2 cup catsup
6 Tbsp lemon juice
1 Tbsp horseradish
1/4 tsp salt
1/2 tsp celery salt
3 drops tabasco sauce

Blend all ingredients and chill.

Cucumber Sauce

1½ cups fish broth
½ cup cream
1 teaspoon lemon juice
Salt and pepper
3 tablespoons oil
4 tablespoons flour
1 tablespoon butter
1 cucumber, grated

1. Heat the stock, add the grated cucumber and simmer together.
2. Heat the oil, sift in the flour, stir and cook together, adding the hot liquid and whisking until smooth.
3. Strain, put on the fire again, add the cream and the butter in small pieces. Season.

Curry Sauce

1 cup milk
1 cup fish stock
1 teaspoon curry powder
2 teaspoons lemon juice
2 teaspoons onion juice
3 tablespoons oil
4 tablespoons flour
1 tablespoon butter
Salt and pepper

1. Heat the milk and fish stock.
2. Heat the oil, add the flour and the curry powder, stir and cook together, adding the hot liquid, whisking it smooth.
3. Add the seasonings.

Dill Sauce

Cucumber, peeled, grated and drained for 1 hour
8 oz (225 g) sour cream
8 oz (225 g) mayonnaise
1 Tbsp fresh lemon juice
1 small clove garlic, minced
1 tsp salt
5 oz (150 g) fresh dill, finely chopped

Combine all the ingredients in a medium bowl. Cover and chill.

Egg Sauce

2 cups milk
3 tablespoons oil
4 tablespoon flour
Salt, paprika
2 hard-boiled eggs, minced
2 teaspoons lemon juice
1 tablespoon butter

1. Scald the milk (don't boil).
2. Heat the oil, stir in the flour, cook together, add the hot milk all at once and whisk until very smooth.
3. Season and add the minced egg.

Hollandaise Sauce

½ cup butter
3 tablespoons flour
1 pint boiling water
3 egg yolks
Lemon juice to taste

1. Melt half the butter, sift in the flour, stir and cook together, adding a pint of boiling water all at once and whisking until very smooth.
2. Begin adding the butter, a small piece at a time, whisking each piece in before adding another, until all the butter is incorporated.
3. Draw aside from the fire and add the beaten egg yolks, just under the boiling point, whisking the sauce as it thickens. *Do not place it where it can boil again or the sauce will curdle.* Add lemon juice to taste.

Note: this sauce should be a thick, yellow sauce like a custard, with slight acidity, yet not sour. There are many other methods for making this sauce, but this is the most simple one.

Horseradish Sauce

1 cup milk
½ cup strong fish stock
2 teaspoons lemon juice
2 tablespoons grated horseradish
3 tablespoons oil
3 tablespoons flour

1 tablespoon butter
Salt and paprika

1. Heat the milk and fish stock.
2. Heat the oil and stir in the flour and cook together, adding the hot liquid all at once and whisking it until smooth.
3. Add horseradish and seasonings.

Horseradish Sauce, Cold

½ cup mayonnaise
2 tablespoons grated horseradish
1 cup whipped cream
Salt and pepper

Mix the ingredients in the order given and set on ice until ready to serve.

Mayonnaise Sauce

Mayonnaise may be considered a type of a sauce. It is also a foundation base for creating more sauces, for example Tartar Sauce or Aioli Sauce. Mustard, horseradish, curry powder, tomato ketchup, anchovy paste can be added to mayonnaise to create new sauces.

½ cup mayonnaise
½ cup sour cream
1 Tbsp lemon juice
2 tsp curry powder

Blend all ingredients together.

Mushroom Sauce

1 cup peeled fresh mushrooms, cut up in pieces
1½ cups milk
½ cup cream
1 egg-white, beaten stiff
Lemon juice to taste
3 tablespoons oil
4 tablespoons flour
2 tablespoons butter
Salt and pepper

1. Melt the butter and cook the mushrooms in it.
2. Heat the milk.

3. Heat the oil, add the flour, stir and cook together, add the hot milk, whisking until smooth.

4. Add the cream and mushrooms, then season.

5. Beat the egg separately, combine with other ingredients and when about to serve the sauce add the egg, making a foamy sauce *which must not be boiled or it will curdle*.

Mustard Sauce

1 tablespoon mustard
1 tablespoon vinegar
1 pint fish stock
Salt and pepper
3 tablespoons oil
3 tablespoons flour
2 egg yolks
⅓ cup cream

1. Heat the fish stock.

2. Heat the oil, stir in the flour and cook together, adding the hot stock all at once and whisking until smooth.

3. Add the cream, then draw aside and add the egg yolks, under the boiling point, whisking them in as they thicken, but not allowing it to approach the boiling point again.

4. Make a paste of mustard and vinegar and add them to sauce. Season and serve.

Orange Sauce

1 cup sugar
3 Tbsp cornstarch
1-1/2 cup orange juice
1/4 cup vinegar
1 tsp finely chopped ginger
1/4 tsp cinnamon
6 whole cloves

Mix sugar and starch in a skillet. Add orange juice, vinegar, ginger. cloves, cinnamon and cook over medium heat, stirring constantly, until thickened.

Oyster Sauce

1 small can of oysters
1 cup milk
½ cup cream
1 teaspoon lemon juice
Salt and pepper
3 tablespoons oil
3 tablespoons flour
1 tablespoon butter

1. Open can of oysters and drain off the juice.
2. Heat the milk and oyster juice.
3. Heat the oil, sift in the flour, stir and cook together, add the hot liquid all at once, whisking until smooth.
4. Add the cream and the oysters, season to taste.

Parsley Cream Sauce

1½ cups milk
½ cup cream
2 tablespoons finely minced parsley
½ lemon juice
3 tablespoons oil
1 tablespoon butter
4 tablespoons flour
Salt and pepper

1. Heat the milk.
2. Heat the oil, stir in flour and cook together, add milk, whisking until smooth. Add the cream, butter and seasonings.
3. When ready to serve, add the minced parsley.

Red Devil

1 cup catsup
1 Tbsp brown sugar
1 Tbsp chopped horseradish
2 Tbsp Worcestersire sauce
1 tsp mustard powder
1/2 tsp chopped ginger
1/2 tsp tabasco sauce
1 Tbsp brandy or rum

Combine all ingredients. Good sauce for dark fleshed fish.

Supreme Sauce

1 pint thick white sauce
1 pint chicken broth
1 cup cream
2 tablespoons butter
1 teaspoon lemon juice
Salt and pepper

1. Simmer the white sauce and chicken broth until reduced by half, be cautious in order to prevent its scorching as it thickens.
2. Add the cream and the butter, whisking it in well, then season.

Note: chopped mushrooms may be added.

Tartar Sauce

1 cup oil
1 egg yolk
Juice ½ lemon
Salt and paprika
1 tablespoon finely minced dill pickle
1 tablespoon onion, finely minced
1 tablespoon parsley, finely minced
1 tablespoon minced capers

1. Put the egg yolk in bowl and begin to drop the oil, a drop at a time, whisking it in well, until the mixture begins to thicken; then add a little lemon juice and return to the oil again, which may be put in more rapidly, a teaspoon at a time, well beaten in until the amount is all used up.

2. Leave the sauce thick and add two tablespoons boiling water to finish the sauce and prevent it from oiling.

3. When cold add the chopped ingredients and cool. Refrigerate.

4. It may be freshened up for use again by adding half a spoon of lemon juice.

Note: making Tartar Sauce is similar to making the mayonnaise and the fastest way to make Tartar Sauce is to add 1 dozen of finely chopped little pickles (gherkins or cornichons) to 1 cup of prepared mayonnaise. You may add one teaspoon of prepared horseradish if available.

Thick White Sauce

3 Tbsp butter or oil
4 Tbsp flour
1 cup milk, hot
¼ tsp salt

1. Melt the butter, stir in the flour, cook together.
2. Add the milk all at once and whisk until smooth.

Note: to make medium white sauce use 2 Tbsp butter (oil), 2 Tbsp flour and 1 cup milk. This sauce may be used with boiled lobster, sweetbreads, chicken cutlets, potatoes, turnips, cabbage, and other similar dishes.

Tomato Cream Sauce

1 cup tomato puree
1 cup milk
½ cup cream
Salt, pepper and a little sugar
3 tablespoons oil
4 tablespoons flour
1 garlic clove, thinly sliced

1. Heat the tomato puree.
2. Heat the cup of milk and cream.
3. Heat the oil, cook the garlic in it, stir in the flour, cook together, adding the hot milk and whisking until smooth.
4. Add the hot tomato and seasonings. This recipe may be doubled, and what is left, with the addition of fish stock or milk, will make an excellent soup for the following day.

Tomato Curry Sauce

1 cup tomato puree
1 cup fish stock
1 tablespoon onion juice
Salt, pepper and a little sugar
3 tablespoons oil
3 tablespoons flour
2 teaspoons curry powder

1. Simmer the tomato puree and fish stock together.
2. Heat the oil, cook the garlic in it, add the flour and curry powder, stir and cook together; add this to the boiling tomato, whisking as it thickens, then season.

Note: you can make your own tomato puree, but it will be much faster to use canned tomato sauce.

To make tomato puree:

½ gallon fresh sliced tomato or 2 large cans
2 large onions, sliced
2 bay leaves
2 garlic cloves, peeled and sliced
4 stalks celery
2 sprigs parsley
2 sprigs thyme
Salt, pepper and sugar to taste

1. Put all the ingredients in a saucepan and simmer gently for 1-2 hours.
2. Cool and strain it. Refrigerate.
3. This is now ready to use in all kinds of sauces calling for tomato.

Velote Sauce

½ cup white fish stock
2 Tbsp butter
2 Tbsp flour
½ cup cream

1. Melt the butter, add the flour, stir and cook together.
2. Add fish stock and slowly cook together for 10 minutes.
3. Warm up the cream and blend all together.

Note: Velote sauce is the foundation sauce for many other fish sauces.

COLD BUTTER SAUCES

Cold butter sauces are much easier to prepare than sauces. They can be prepared beforehand and kept in a refrigerator, unlike some sauces, for example Hollandaise, that does not freeze well. Then, at serving time, put a teaspoon of butter or as much as you desire on a hot fish. If the fish is cold, you can melt down the butter and poured it over the fish. *When making a butter sauce, the first step is to cream the butter.* This is a common procedure in baking. The difference is that we don't add sugar to butter when making fish sauces.

To cream butter: leave the cold butter sticks for one hour at room temperature. Put the butter in a bowl and beat it with a mixer or whisk manually.

Anchovy Butter

2 tsp lemon juice
1 tsp anchovy paste
3 Tbsp butter, melted
Dash paprika
1 Tbsp chopped parsley

Cream the butter, adding the lemon juice a little at a time and the parsley.

Curry Butter

¼ cup butter
½ tsp (or to flavor) curry powder

Mix together and refrigerate.

Dill Butter

½ cup butter
1 Tbsp lemon juice
1 Tbsp finely chopped dill

Cream the butter, adding the lemon juice a little at a time and the dill. Refrigerate.

Garlic Butter

½ cup butter
2 Tbsp very finely chopped garlic
1 Tbsp lemon juice
Salt and pepper to taste

Cream the butter, adding the lemon juice a little at a time and the garlic. Refrigerate.

Ginger Butter

½ cup butter
2 Tbsp very finely chopped garlic
1 Tbsp lemon juice
1 tsp finely chopped fresh ginger
Salt and pepper to taste

Cream the butter, adding the lemon juice a little at a time and the garlic and ginger. Refrigerate.

Horseradish Butter

½ cup butter
1 Tbsp prepared horseradish

Cream the butter, adding horseradish. Refrigerate.

Lemon Butter

4 Tbsp butter
2 tsp. lemon juice

Cream the butter, working in the lemon juice. Refrigerate.

Parsley Butter

½ cup butter
1 Tbsp lemon juice
1 Tbsp finely chopped parsley

Cream the butter, adding the lemon juice a little at a time and the parsley. Refrigerate.

Wasabi Butter

½ cup butter
1 tsp Wasabi (Wasabi is a green Japanese horseradish).

Cream the butter, adding Wasabi. Refrigerate.

Appendix

Brine Tables and How to Use Them

If you come across a recipe and you would like to determine what is the strength of the brine, just follow the two steps:

1. Find the percent of salt by weight in the solution: weight of salt/(weight of salt plus weight of water), then multiply the result by 100%.
2. Look up the tables and find the corresponding salometer degree.

For example let's find the strength of the brine that is mentioned in many recipes and calls for adding 1 pound of salt to 1 gallon of water (8.33 pounds).

% salt by weight = 1lb of salt/1 lb of salt + 8.33 lbs (1 gallon) of water = 0.1071
0.1071 x 100 % = 10.71 % of salt
Looking in the table at Column 2 (percent salt by weight) we can see that 10.71% corresponds to 40 ½ degrees.

Another popular brine is made by adding 3/4 cup of salt (219 g) to 1 gallon (3.8 liters) of water

219 g / 219 + 3800 g = 0.05
0.05 x 100 = 5% of salt

Looking in the table at Column 2 (percent salt by weight) we can see that 5% corresponds to 19 degrees.

Adding salt to water and checking the reading with a salometer is a rather time consuming method. You can make brine much faster by using tables, the way professionals do. For example we want 22 degrees brine to cure chicken. Follow the 22 degree row to the right you will see in Column 3 that 0.513 lb of salt is added to 1 gallon of water to make 22 degree brine. To make 80 degree brine mix 2.229 lbs of salt with 1 gallon of water. Then check it with your salinometer and add/deduct more water or salt to get a perfect reading.

If you end up with not enough brine, make some more. If you think you may need just 1/2 gallon more of 80 degree brine, take 1/2 gallon of water and add 1/2 of salt that the table asks for. In this case looking at 80 degree brine (Column 1), going to the right you can see that in Column 3 the amount of the needed salt is 2.229 lb. Yes, but this amount is added to 1 gallon of water to create 80 degree brine. Because we use only 1/2 gallon now, this amount of salt needs to be halved: 2.229 lb/2 = 1.11 lb. In other words if we add 1.11 lbs of salt to 1/2 gallon of water we will also create 80 degree brine.

Let's say you need about 10 gallons of 60 degrees SAL brine (15.8% salt) to cure ham. Locate 60 degrees SAL in Column 1 and then go across to Column 3 where it is stated that 1.567 pounds salt/gallon of water is needed. Multiplying 1.567 (pounds salt/gallon of water x 10 gallons of water gives us 15.67 lbs of salt. This is how much salt needs to be added to 10 gallons of water to make 60 degrees SAL brine.

Sodium Chloride (Salt) Brine Tables For Brine at 60° F (15° C) in US Gallons

Salometer Degrees	% of Salt by Weight	Pounds of Salt per US Gallon of Water
0	0.000	0.000
1	0.264	0.022
2	0.526	0.044
3	0.792	0.066
4	1.056	0.089
5	1.320	0.111
6	1.584	0.134
7	1.848	0.157
8	2.112	0.180
9	2.376	0.203
10	2.640	0.226
11	2.903	0.249
12	3.167	0.272
13	3.431	0.296
14	3.695	0.320
15	3.959	0.343
16	4.223	0.367
17	4.487	0.391
18	4.751	0.415
19	5.015	0.440
20	5.279	0.464
21	5.543	0.489
22	5.807	**0.513**
23	6.071	0.538
24	6.335	0.563
25	6.599	0.588
26	6.863	0.614
27	7.127	0.639
28	7.391	0.665
29	7.655	0.690
30	7.919	0.716

31	8.162	0.742
32	8.446	0.768
33	8.710	0.795
34	8.974	0.821
35	9.238	0.848
36	9.502	0.874
37	9.766	0.901
38	10.030	0.928
39	10.294	0.956
40	10.588	0.983
41	10.822	1.011
42	11.086	1.038
43	11.350	1.066
44	11.614	1.094
45	11.878	1.123
46	12.142	1.151
47	12.406	1.179
48	12.670	1.208
49	12.934	1.237
50	13.198	1.266
51	13.461	1.295
52	13.725	1.325
53	13.989	1.355
54	14.253	1.384
55	14.517	1.414
56	14.781	1.444
57	15.045	1.475
58	15.309	1.505
59	15.573	1.536
60	15.837	**1.567**
61	16.101	1.598
62	16.365	1.630
63	16.629	1.661
64	16.893	1.693
65	17.157	1.725

66	17.421	1.757
67	17.685	1.789
68	17.949	1.822
69	18.213	1.854
70	18.477	1.887
71	18.740	1.921
72	19.004	1.954
73	19.268	1.988
74	19.532	2.021
75	19.796	2.056
76	20.060	2.090
77	20.324	2.124
78	20.588	2.159
79	20.852	2.194
80	21.116	**2.229**
81	21.380	2.265
82	21.644	2.300
83	21.908	2.336
84	22.172	2.372
85	22.436	2.409
86	22.700	2.446
87	22.964	2.482
88	23.228	2.520
89	23.492	2.557
90	23.756	2.595
91	24.019	2.633
92	24.283	2.671
93	24.547	2.709
94	24.811	2.748
95	25.075	2.787
96	25.339	2.826
97	25.603	2.866
98	25.867	2.908
99	26.131	2.948
100	26.395	2.986

- Seawater contains approximately 3.695% of salt which corresponds to 14 degrees salometer reading.
- At 100 degrees brine is fully saturated and contains 26.395% of salt.
- 1 US gallon of water weighs 8.33 lb.
- 1 US gallon = 3.8 liters = 3.8 kilograms.
- Bear in mind that when you add Cure #1 to your solution (it contains 93.75 % salt) you will be changing the strength of the brine, especially at higher degrees. Simply subtract this amount from the salt given by the tables.

Salinometer readings are calibrated to give a correct indication when the brine is at 60° F temperature. Each brine tester will have its own instructions for temperature compensation but the basic rule of thumb says that for every 10° F the brine is above 60° F, one degree should be added to the reading before using table. If the brine is below 60° F subtract 1 degree for each 10° F from the observed salinometer reading before using table.

For example, if a salinometer indicates 70 degrees brine and the brine's temperature is 40° F, the corrected salinometer reading would be 68 degrees (for each 10° F below 60° F, one salinometer degree is subtracted). If the brine temperature is 80° F and the salinometer indicates 40 degrees, the corrected reading would be 82 degrees SAL (for each 10° F above 60° F, one salinometer degree is added). These are very small differences which are of bigger importance for a meat plant curing huge amounts of meat at one time. Needless to say a thermometer is needed too.

Note: There is another set of brine tables for UK Gallons (UK imperial gallon = 4.54 liters) and it can be looked up on Internet.

Concrete Block Smoker *(Reprinted from Meat Smoking and Smokehouse Design)*

An excellent smoker can be built without any tools in e few hours by using standard 8" x 8" x 16" concrete blocks.

Fig. A1 Concrete block.

This is a very flexible design and imagine that you are building a smoker like a child who is erecting a house using little building blocks. This is how this smoker is built and the only difference is that the blocks are slightly bigger. The required materials are either lying around for free or are available from a building supply store.

A firm support base is recommended and square patio stones of 12", 16", or 18" that are available at garden centers can be used, however, the smoker can be built right on a bare ground. Just grade it well so it is leveled. The construction does not require using mortar, just arranging blocks in the manner that will be most practical. A separate fire pit built from blocks is attached to the smokehouse. This way the entire smoking chamber can be utilized for smoking meats and the process is easy to control. A permanent structure can be made, but a strong suggestion is to try it out a few times.

side view   front view

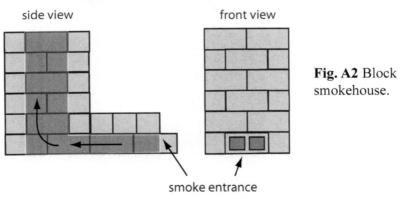

Fig. A2 Block smokehouse.

smoke entrance

The easiest and fastest way to support the smokesticks is to place them directly on top of the smoker. The sticks should be 1" in diameter as they act as spacers now, separating the top of the smoker from the cardboard or wooden cover that rests on it. This creates ample space for the smoke to exit from the smoker.

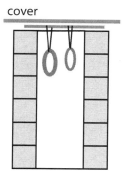

Fig. A3 Smokesticks on top.

To control exit of smoke an old potato burlap sack has been used in the past. Of course a flattened piece of cardboard or a piece of plywood can be used as well.

Construction Details

The block laying style repeats itself, uneven layers 1, 3, 5 have one pattern, even layers 2, 4, 6 have another one. There are 5 blocks in #1 level, all others require 6 blocks. In a six floor configuration *a total of 36 blocks are used for the smoker and 7 blocks for the fire pit.* Neither masonry bricks, mortar, half blocks or any tools are needed. As the fire pit is on the same plane as the smoker, in order to achieve enough draft, the smoker is built of six floors and is 48" high which makes it a comfortable height to work with. It will also work if the height is limited to 5 block levels (40") and if more draft is needed, an extra floor can be added in a matter of minutes.

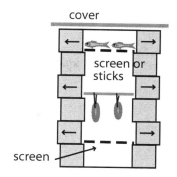

Fig. A4 Smokesticks on blocks.

Top view at smoker & firepit

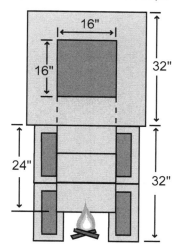

Fig. A5 Top view.

The blocks can be spaced so that every other row can have two blocks projecting inward from the wall on each side of the smoker. This arrangement creates support for the smokesticks, screens or racks.

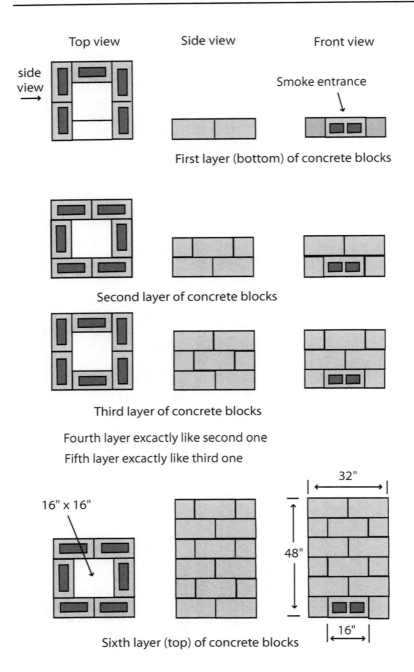

Top view   Side view   Front view

First layer (bottom) of concrete blocks

Second layer of concrete blocks

Third layer of concrete blocks

Fourth layer excactly like second one

Fifth layer excactly like third one

Sixth layer (top) of concrete blocks

Fig. A6 Top, side and front views.

Fire Pit

There are only 7 blocks needed to construct the fire pit which is freely attached to the front wall. Any little smoke coming from the connection is negligible as long as there is smoke coming out of the chamber. A wet towel can be placed over the connection where the fire pit and smoker come together. A fire pit may be attached to the smoker with a mortar. As the concrete block is not designed to withhold high temperatures it is to be expected that once in a while one of the fire pit concrete blocks might crack. Obviously, the most practical solution is to replace it with a different one.

A long stem thermometer can be inserted between blocks or through the top cover. The temperature control and amount of heat generated is obtained by moving burning wood closer or away from the entrance to the smoker. This is a fully functional and easy to operate smoker capable of producing smoked meats of the highest quality and it should not be judged by its looks. Its useful inside space is only 0.7 cubic foot (0.18 cubic meter) smaller than that of a typical metal drum, providing that we could use all of the drum's space for smoking. Resting smokesticks on two separate levels creates enough capacity to smoke about 22 lbs (10 kg) of meats.

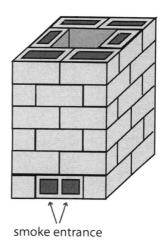

smoke entrance

Fig. A7 Top view.

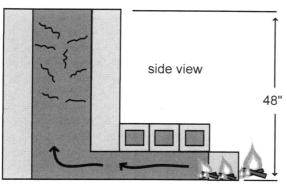

side view

48"

Fig. A8 Smoker with attached fire pit.

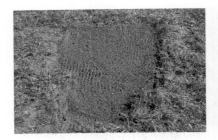

Photo A.1 Preparing the ground.

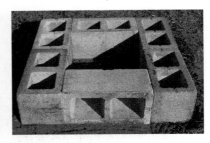

Photo A.2 The first level.

Photo A.3 The second level.

Photo A.4 Five levels, 40" high.

Photo A.5 Front view.

Photo A.6 Side view.

Photo A.7 Firebox channel.

Photo A.8 Top view, fire flames.

Photo A.9 Burlap cloth allows the right amount of smoke to exit.

The firebox channel does not have to be necessarily covered with concrete blocks, a sheet of metal will work good. It will heat coffee or soup when the weather is cold.

The principle of using concrete blocks can be applied for building much bigger units as described on the following pages.

Masonry Smokehouse # 5695 *(Reprinted from Meat Smoking and Smokehouse Design)*

The following smokehouse was designed in 1965 by the North Dakota State University and the U.S. Dept. of Agriculture. This is a big walk-in smokehouse requiring a foundation reaching below the frost line. This is the depth where water can still be found frozen depending on a particular geographical location.

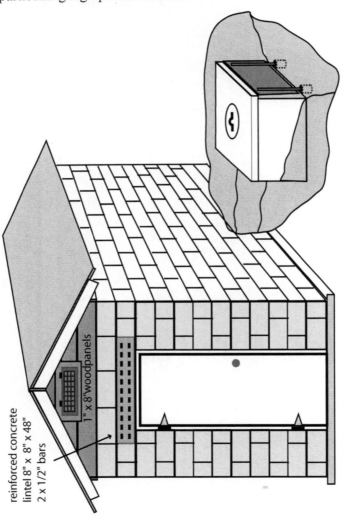

Fig. A9 General view.

This is a classical design of a smokehouse that has been used in Europe and later in the USA for centuries. About 10' high, ventilation on both sides, # 30 mesh screen on the inside and a hinged door on the outside. A removable utility bench inside and the barrel with salt in the corner. The smokehouse is built using standard size concrete blocks 8" x 8" x 16" which make the project inexpensive and easy to complete. It is almost like building a small house foundation, concrete walls and a wooden roof that can be covered with shingles. The floor is made of 4" concrete, the door is covered on the inside with sheet metal. The advantage of this design is an excellent insulation and a very strong design.

The smokehouse is well insulated as there is air inside the concrete blocks. The top blocks can be filled with attic insulation to make it even tighter.

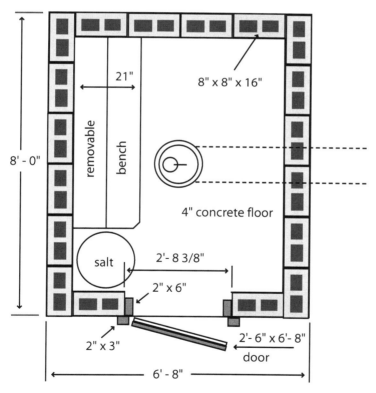

Fig. A10 Floor plan.

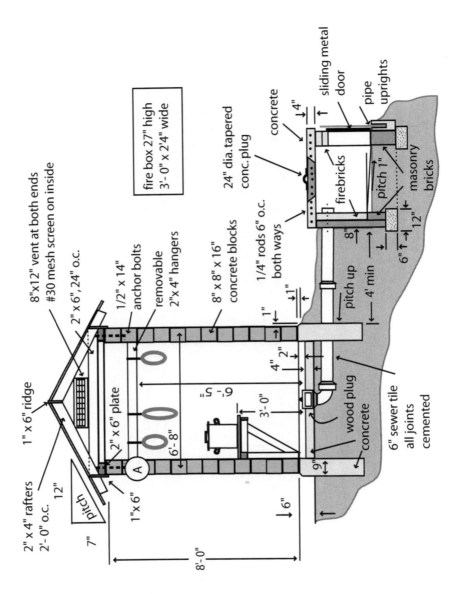

Fig. A11 Cross section.

This type of smokehouse may be an overkill for a home sausage maker but becomes a very attractive proposition for someone who wants to make products for sale. Propane burners will provide all heat that is required and the unit can be placed in a remote area.

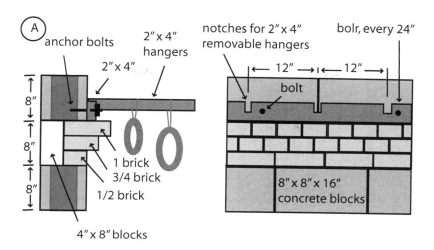

Fig. A12 Support for hangers.

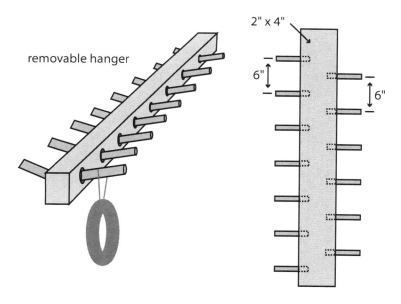

Fig. A13 Hangers.

This type of design has proven itself for hundreds of years and cannot be beaten. Many professional butchers use their own brick layered smokehouses with a great deal of success.

Useful Links and Resources

Equipment and Supplies

The Sausage Maker Inc., 1500 Clinton St., Building 123, Buffalo, NY 14206, 888-490-8525; 716-824-5814
www.sausagemaker.com

Allied Kenco Sales, 26 Lyerly #1, Houston, TX 77022
713-691-2935; 800-356-5189
www.alliedkenco.com

Walton's Inc., 3639 N. Comotara, Wichita, KS 67226-1304
(316) 262-0651; Fax: (316) 262-5136
www.waltonsinc.com

Meat Processing Products, PO Box 5755, Incline Village, NV 89450
(877) 231-8589; Fax: (775)-548-9848
www.meatprocessingproducts.com

The Sausage Source, 3 Henniker Road Hillsboro, NH 03244
(603) 464-6275
www.sausagesource.com

Halfords, 8629-126th Ave, Edmonton, Alberta T5B 1G8, Canada
(780) 474-4989; Fax: (780) 477-3489
www.halfordsmailorder.com

Tejas Smokers, P.O. Box 4158, Houston, Texas 77210-4158
(713) 932-6438; Fax: (713) 222-6096
www.tejassmokers.com

Smoke Daddy Inc., 54 Le Baron, Waukegan IL, 60085
Phone: (847) 336-1329
www.smokedaddyinc.com

Index

Other Books by Stanley and Adam Marianski

Home Production of Quality Meats And Sausages bridges the gap that exists between highly technical textbooks and the requirements of the typical hobbyist. The book covers topics such as curing and making brines, smoking meats and sausages, making special sausages such as head cheeses, blood and liver sausages, hams, bacon, butts, loins, safety and more...

ISBN: 978-0-9824267-3-9

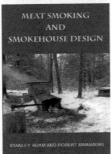

Meat Smoking & Smokehouse Design explains differences between grilling, barbecuing and smoking. There are extensive discussions of curing as well as the particulars about smoking sausages, meat, fish, poultry and wild game.

ISBN: 978-0-9824267-0-8

The Art of Making Fermented Sausages shows readers how to control meat acidity and removal of moisture, choose proper temperatures for fermenting, smoking and drying, understand and control fermentation process, choose proper starter cultures and make traditional or fast-fermented products, choose proper equipment, and much more...

ISBN: 978-0-9824267-1-5

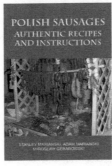

Polish Sausages contains government recipes that were used by Polish meat plants between 1950-1990. These recipes come from government manuals that were never published before, which are now revealed in great detail.

ISBN: 978-0-9824267-2-2

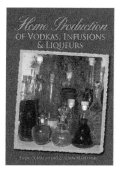

Sauerkraut, Kimchi, Pickles and Relishes teaches you how to lead a healthier and longer life. Most commercially produced foods are heated and that step eliminates many of the beneficial bacteria, vitamins and nutrients. However, most of the healthiest vegetables can be fermented without thermal processing. The book explains in simple terms the fermentation process, making brine, pickling and canning.

ISBN: 978-0-9836973-2-9

Making Healthy Sausages reinvents traditional sausage making by introducing a completely new way of thinking. The reader will learn how to make a product that is nutritional and healthy, yet delicious to eat. The collection of 80 recipes provides a valuable reference on the structure of reduced fat products.

ISBN: 978-0-9836973-0-5

The Amazing Mullet offers information that has been gathered through time and experience. Successful methods of catching, smoking and cooking fish are covered in great depth and numerous filleting, cleaning, cooking and smoking practices are reviewed thoroughly. In addition to mullet recipes, detailed information on making fish cakes, ceviche, spreads and sauces are also included.

ISBN: 978-0-9824267-8-4

Home Production of Vodkas, Infusions & Liqueurs is a guide for making quality alcohol beverages at home. The book adopts factory methods of making spirits but without the need for any specialized equipment. A different type of alcohol beverage can be produced from the same fruit and the authors explain in simple terms all necessary rules.

ISBN: 978-0-9836973-4-3

Home Canning Meat, Poultry, Fish and Vegetables explains in simple language the science of canning low-acid foods such as meat, poultry, fish ans vegetables and reveals the procedures that are used by the canning industry. The material is based on the U.S. government requirements as specified in the Code of Federal Regulations and the relevant links are listed. After studying the book, a newcomer to the art of canning will be able to safely process foods at home in both glass and metal containers.

ISBN: 978-0-9836973-7-4

Printed in Great Britain
by Amazon

76503849R00154